On Staying Awake

Marie-Louise von Franz, Honorary Patron

**Studies in Jungian Psychology
by Jungian Analysts**

Daryl Sharp, General Editor

ON STAYING AWAKE

Getting older and bolder

Another Jungian Romance

DARYL SHARP

For my sons, David Richard and Benjamin Nicholas,
and grandsons Devon, Dylan and Julian Emery.

The events, characters and situations in this book are neither wholly true nor entirely fictional. Rather they are embroideries on reality, which, after all, is the nature of any romance. Names, of course, have been changed, mostly.

Library and Archives Canada Cataloguing in Publication

Sharp, Daryl, 1936-
On staying awake: getting older and bolder; another
Jungian romance / Daryl Sharp.

(Studies in Jungian psychology by Jungian analysts; 115)

Includes bibliographical references and index.

1-894574-16-8

1. Self-actualization (Psychology). 2. Jungian psychology.

I. Title. II. Series.

BF175.S4925 2006   158.1   C2005-907008-0

INNER CITY BOOKS
Box 1271, Station Q, Toronto, ON M4T 2P4, Canada
Telephone (416) 927-0355 / Fax (416) 924-1814

Web site: www.innercitybooks.net
E-mail:admin@innercitybooks.net

Honorary Patron: Marie-Louise von Franz.
Publisher and General Editor: Daryl Sharp.
Senior Editor: Victoria B. Cowan.

INNER CITY BOOKS was founded in 1980 to promote the
understanding and practical application of the work of C.G. Jung.

Cover: *The Replica of Willendorf/post-prehistoric.* 784 lightbulbs 90" x 40" x 40".
Jerry Pethick, sculptor, Hornby Island, British Columbia, Canada, 1982. Photo courtesy
Bob Cain, Hornby Island. See also page 117.

Printed and bound in Canada by University of Toronto Press Inc.

CONTENTS

See final pages for more books by Daryl Sharp and other Inner City titles

The breeze at dawn has secrets to tell you.
Don't go back to sleep.
You must ask for what you really want.
Don't go back to sleep.
People are going back and forth across the doorsill
Where the two worlds touch.
The door is round and open.
Don't go back to sleep.
—Rumi.

romance, noun & adjective, & verb intransitive:
1. Prose or (rarely) verse tale with scenes and incidents remote from everyday life; class of literature consisting of such tales; set of facts, episode, love affair, etc., suggesting such tales by its strangeness or moving nature; atmosphere characterizing such tales, sympathetic imaginativeness.
2. exaggeration, picturesque falsehood.
3. short piece of simple character.
4. to exaggerate or distort the truth, draw the long-bow.
—*Concise Oxford Dictionary.*

Preface

After finishing my last book with Adam Brillig, *Not the Big Sleep,* I thought that was it, I was done for. I felt I had nothing more to say and that I would never write anything else.

But as the accolades rolled in—"insightful and witty," "informative and readable," "changed my life," "shamelessly clever," "charmingly understated," "totally awesome," and so on—I got a swelled-up head and in spite of myself began thinking of what I might write next.

Okay, so I got carried away with my own self-importance and the desire to be appreciated, loved, what have you. Who is invulnerable to all that? Not me, that's for sure. I have a prototypical (call it archetypal, why not) narcissistic writing personality disorder (NWPD)—so proud of what I've created that I can barely shut up about it. This soon becomes tiresome to friends, especially as it extends to browbeating them into reading my work. I mean, they have their own busy lives! I just wish they didn't.

However, I do so like Prof. Adam Brillig. I think the world would be a poorer place without him. And without me, think about it, where would he be?

My loverNot, dear Nurse Pam, also featured in *Not the Big Sleep,* was beside herself. "Forget Harry Potter and *The Da Vinci Code,"* she cried. "Don't even think about *Lord of the Rings.* You are a world-famous author, the prince of Jungian romance. You have the goods and the momentum. Go for it."

Well, with that kind of backing, who wouldn't?

*

The above thoughts came to me a few months ago when I was in a hospital bed recovering from bifemoral arterial bypass surgery, occasioned on account of the lack of circulation in my lower limbs, itself the result of plaque build-up in my arteries, probably due to smoking about forty cigarettes a day for fifty years. Of course I rolled my own with Drum tobacco—it gave me something to do with my hands when there were no lovelies around—but still.

Being in the hospital was no fun at all, nor was the food. I'm a meat and potatoes kinda guy, but they weren't on the menu. I lost twenty pounds because I could rarely eat what was served: puréed prunes, soy burgers, cauliflower soup, cream of wheat with raisins, low-cal tapioca pudding, minced carrots, tofu cakes, tangerine mousse and so on. All very healthy, I'm sure, but what got me in there in the first place was not eating what was good for me; so I still didn't, nothing new about that.

But the worst, the very worst, was what they cavalierly called "scrambled egg beaters"—which sounds faintly like something you do or eat of a misty morning in England when hunting foxes, or maybe a Welsh variant of eggs Benedict. But it's none of that. Give up? Well, it's eggs cooked and dehydrated to a powder that is later reconstructed with hot water, and then they use an ice cream scoop to plop some of that yellow gloop on your plate beside a sprig of parsley. Yuk, I mean totally disgusting. Scrambled egg beaters were far worse than the surgery, from which I recovered right away, give or take a minor stroke or two, which I will tell you about a little later.

Talk about hospital food. Every morning I was presented with a sheet of paper detailing what was available to eat the next day. "Please cross off foods you cannot eat," it said at the top. Well, I changed "cannot" to "will not" and drew a red X through the whole page. More than once I wrote in the margin, "You can put this stuff where the sun don't shine. Bring me fish and chips or a hamburger, thanks," which they never did—so much for the patient comes first.

Meanwhile, my intrepid older brother sent me a get-well card that light-heartedly detailed "things to do while you're in the hospital." There was "fluff up your pillow and pretend you're resting on a cloud," and "make a list of all the chores you're getting out of," but the one I liked best was "Eat dessert first," which I did religiously, and then after a time I ate nothing else. I became so weak from malnutrition that I even stopped leering at the nurses, theretofore all the more erotic to my mind for being veiled in their shapeless hospital greens.

Well, apparently my loss of libido was noticed, for after a covert meeting in the broom closet—to which I was not invited, bet your bottom dollar on that—the nurses determined to inflict on me a procedure known in medical-speak by the code S-G-N (stomach-gastric-nose). What it is, is nothing to guess about. I'll tell you straight out: they <u>thrust</u> (there is no kinder word for it) a long tube into one nostril and slowly push it all the way down to your stomach as they pour gruel into your mouth and shouting, "Swallow! Swallow!" while you gag and thrash about and feel like throwing up. They did this to me more than once, claiming it was for my own good, and maybe it was, but they stopped when I howled and jabbed a finger at the large sign on the wall:

WE CARE ABOUT YOUR PAIN

1. *Relief of pain helps recovery.*
2. *Don't let your pain get out of control—tell someone early.*
3. *The best pain management involves you, your family, and the health care team.*

Anyway, I guess they didn't hold it against me, because a few days later, just before they transferred me to rehab on account of the teensy weensy stroke, a bunch of pretty nurses gathered at the foot of my bed and sang, "He's a jolly good fellow." Then they presented me with a heart-shaped red pillow the size of a snowshoe. "Hold it close against your tummy," cooed one of them, "so when you cough you won't pop any staples." And she demonstrated; wow, what a tummy, what staples.

My loverNot friend Nurse Pam thinks I should turn *Not the Big Sleep* into a stage play. Well, I can tell you I'm nothing loath! But I never wrote a play before, and all the books I've written are little more than screeds in disguise. So I'll certainly need some help. And while you're working on that, spare a wee thought for this poor wretched gecko who has set himself the daunting task of writing yet another Jungian romance.

Traversing the Void.
Wall piece by Canadian sculptor Jerry Pethick, 1986-1990.
(galvanized metal, enameled steel, mirror, glass, plywood, aluminum
frame, glass fluorescent tube.) Author's collection.

1
Introduction

It was my first night in rehab. I was completely disoriented. I wasn't even aware that I had been moved from one hospital to another until my son Dave brought me up to speed.

"You were raving in the ambulance!" he said, wringing his hands. "You said you were the leader of an intergalactic probe to determine how advanced the people on earth were! Dad, that's pretty creepy!"

I replied: "I expect it was wishful thinking"—and surely it was, for frankly I could not imagine a people more backward than earthlings, who from all accounts are working overtime to destroy life on our planet. Apparently there were other dreams that threw into doubt my mental stability, but I don't recall them.

A couple of nurses plumped my pillows, stroked my feet and cheeks and adjusted my IV; then I slipped into a fitful sleep (or call it a coma, why not), interrupted by visions of aliens who all looked remarkably like my mentor, Professor Adam Brillig: old, bald, dwarfish and misshapen. I took this to be a good sign because, as noted earlier, I have a good feeling about Adam Brillig. It's not just that I think he's wiser than anyone else I know; more important, he accepts me as I am—no ifs, ands or buts; and I return the favor, as it were and if it is.

All kidding aside, ever since I had that little stroke after the surgery, my executive or so-called higher functions, both abstract and concrete—ruled they tell me by the frontal lobe, which according to the CT scan was hit the worst—had been fuzzy. I shuffled and forgot what I was supposed to do next. I washed my hands in mid-air. My speech wasn't slurred, but I often couldn't recall the words for ordinary things, like window, ceiling, towel, paper clips and more. And a couple of times I wandered in the night out of sight of the ward's video surveillance, which apparently freaked somebody out, because soon after that they shipped me off to St. John's rehab hospital in north Toronto (gifted to the province by the Sisters of St. John the Divine), where I was taken in hand by a team of lovelies whose mandate was apparently to cure me with tough love, which meant waking me up at any hour for a pill or a needle or even a friendly "how you doin'?" I thought I could have done without any of that if they would just let me sleep, but I wasn't in charge and for all I know they saved my life.

At St. John's I soon settled into a regular routine. Every morning I went down to the lobby to pick up a newspaper from the vending machine. In the evening I played Scrabble with the octogenarian lovely in the next room or joined the heavy hittters for bingo in Great Hall (once I won a back scratcher with a full house). In between medical appointments I read detective novels or tried to get the television to work. Of course they don't let you sleep in hospitals, maybe in case you never wake up. If they're not taking your blood, they're offering you food or changing the sheets or whatnot. The last person to get any sleep in a hospital was Rip van Winkle, and you know what happened to him.

I can tell you, physio was a blast. I was in the care of a cute little Jamaican woman in her twenties. Her skin was smooth as 18% cream. Petula was her name; Petal I thought of her.

"Mr. Razor," she would say, stopwatch in hand, "I'm going to time you walking up these steps backward, one at a time. When you get to the top step you honk! Understand? You honk! Can you honk?"

I honked, just to show I was not hearing impaired. So we did that exercise and apparently I did okay because we moved on to the next task, which was to walk a straight line for twenty seconds without falling over—like a roadside Breathalyzer. I managed that, and then came the Big One.

"Now," said Ms. Petal, "I want you to touch your nose with your right index finger, then touch my nose with yours—ten times in a minute. Do it, go guy!"

I did like that one and even got in a lick or two. She smiled and said I passed.

My occupational therapist, Wendy, was Puerto Rican. She was quite as nubile as Petal, but not so forgiving. She laid out a sheaf of papers and

asked me to sort them according to which were bills needing to be paid;
then she told me to write the checks. I did so, but alas, I included one that
had already been paid. I lost some marks for that.

Wendy said: "Never mind, that wasn't easy. You got 87%, which is
really great!!"

I said: "I'm very tired and you're so lovely. Can we lie down now and
hold hands?"

"We're almost finished," said Wendy, frowning. "Please don't crap
out on me! I'm still in training."

She took me then to the next stage in the O.T.'s chamber of horrors,
which was to hang by my thumbs over a pit of sulfuric acid while listening to Leonard Cohen sing "Suzanne" for twenty minutes. Well, that's
how it felt. I did even worse on that test, which is to say I failed. The
next task was to count backward from 100, subtracting 7 at a time. I did
that with ease; well, I do have a degree in math.

Then Wendy took me into the hospital kitchenette and asked me to
prepare a meal from start to eat. I opted to make an omelet and a salad,
and did just fine until we were leaving, at which point Wendy pointed
out that I'd forgotten to turn the burner off.

Silly buggers! Well I can tell you, I lost marks for that, big time, and
got a tongue lashing to boot.

Wendy said: "You moron, you villainous wordmonger, you wretched,
amoral flirt!"

That really hurt. I said: "Pardon me, I'm not quite myself. I am very
sorry if I have inadvertently offended you in some way. I've had a
stroke, you see, and my mind may be irreparably damaged. Remember
the first rule of nursing: Do no harm. I'm a patient. Aren't you supposed
to treat me kindly and with respect? Have you no heart?"

Wendy winced, but then shook a finger at me and struck a pose that I
thought was meant to be intimidating. This did not work on me, for in
my professional life as a psychoanalyst, I have survived more than a few
projections of women's inner demons. I simply took her in my arms and
told her she was the most beautiful midget I'd ever known. (She was just
four foot six, you see, but every inch a winner; I wouldn't mis-speak

about that.)

"I could love you," I declared.

Wendy collapsed in my arms. "Do with me what you will," she said.

Well, would that I could. But I was only up to going back to bed. My staples weren't even all out yet. What I was after was freedom, and when Wendy discharged me from O.T. I was close to it. It only took another week or so before I was pronounced fit enough to go home—well, on condition that there was someone, a "responsible grown-up" in med-speak, to stay with me overnight, just in case I fell down the stairs or slipped in the shower or took it into my head to do something really loony like go out to sleep in the snow.

That "someone" turned out to be many different persons, including various lovelies, one or other of my kids, charitable friends, and so on. I did bask in the attention and my appetite returned. My stomach incisions began to heal and hair grew over.

Over the next little while I saw more than one vascular surgeon who pronounced me completely healed. The head honcho of occupational therapists put me though some tests and said he found no hangover from the stroke. The Ministry of Transportation then reinstated my driver's license, and with my dear little egg-yolk gold Volkswagen in the drive-way I no longer felt like an invalid.

Four weeks passed. My stomach still hurt, but only a little. I could walk without limping and without a cane, and I could almost make love without crying. Who could ask for anything more? (Well, I did miss the Scotch, which I had reluctantly agreed to do without for awhile.)

*

Let's talk a bit about projection. It's one of my favorite subjects and I'm caught by it more often than I care to admit.

Jung was among the first to point out that we are constantly projecting the contents of our unconscious into our environment; which is to say, we see unacknowledged aspects of ourselves in other people. In this way we create a series of imaginary relationships that often have little or nothing to do with the persons we relate to.

We are naturally inclined to believe that the world is as we see it, that people are who we imagine them to be. However, we soon learn that this is not so, because other people frequently turn out to be quite different from the way we thought they were. If they are not particularly close, we think no more about it. If this experience involves a lover or someone we are otherwise intimate with, we may be devastated.

I recently talked about this with my mentor Adam Brillig.

"It is quite normal," said Adam, "for unconscious contents to be projected. That's life. Projection has generally had a bad press, but in its positive sense it creates an agreeable bridge between people, facilitating friendship and communication. Like the persona—the "I" we show to others—projection greases the wheels of social intercourse. And as with complexes, life would be a whole lot duller without projection."

You can also project onto things. This used to be known as having a fetish and was generally considered to be unhealthy. People laughed at you if you had a fascination for, say, shoes or buttons or hats or, well, elephants. They may still laugh, of course, but nowadays some of us know that such things have a symbolic, psychological meaning.

There is passive projection and there is active projection. Passive projection is completely automatic and unintentional. Our eyes catch another's across a crowded room and we are smitten, head over heels, or take an instant dislike. We may know nothing about that person; in fact the less we know, the easier it is to project. We fill the void with ourselves.

Active projection is also known as empathy. You feel yourself into the other's shoes by imagining what he or she is going through. This is an essential ability for any therapist. Without it there is a long succession of boring days with uninteresting people who have unimaginable problems. With it, you're on the edge.

There is a thin line between empathy and identification. Identification presupposes no separation between subject and object, no difference between me and the other person. We are two peas in a pod. What is good for me must be good for him—or her. Many relationships run aground on this mistaken notion. It is the motivation for much well-meaning advice to others, and the premise of any therapeutic system relying on suggestion or adaptation to collectively sanctioned behavior and ideals.

Therapy conducted on this basis does more harm than good. That is why Jung insisted that those in training to become analysts must have a thorough personal analysis before being let loose. Only through an intimate knowledge of my own complexes and predispositions can I know where I end and the other begins. And even then I can't always be sure. When someone whose psychology is similar to mine shows up—like Norman, who comes up here later—I really have to be careful.

In relationships, identification is as common as potatoes and always spells trouble. Jung describes what can happen:

> When a person complains that he is always on bad terms with his wife or the people whom he loves, and that there are terrible scenes or resistances between them, you will see when you analyze this person that he has an attack of hatred. He has been living in *participation mystique* with those he loves. He has spread himself over other people until he has become identical with them, which is a violation of the principle of individuality. Then they have resistances naturally, in order to keep themselves apart. I say:
> "Of course it is most regrettable that you always get into trouble, but don't you see what you are doing? You love somebody, you identify with them, and of course you prevail against the objects of your love and repress them by your very self-evident identity. You handle them as if they were yourself, and naturally there will be resistances. It is a violation of the individuality of those people, and it is a sin against your own individuality. Those resistances are a most useful and important instinct: you have resistances, scenes, and disappointments so that you may become finally conscious of yourself, and then hatred is no more."[1]

When you identify with another person, your emotional well-being is intimately linked with the mood of that person and his or her attitude toward you. It's a classic double bind. You can't function independently and your dependence has the effect of making the other person responsible for how *you* feel. More: you have a relationship that is psychologically no different from that between parent and child. Worse: at any

---

[1] *The Psychology of Kundalini Yoga: Notes of the Seminar Given in 1932 by C.G. Jung,* p. 7.

given moment it is hard to tell who is parent and who is child. That is the picture of what psychologists call codependency.

Codependence is psychologically appropriate between parent and child, but it doesn't work between adults. Neither can make a move without double-thinking the effect on the other, which automatically inhibits the self-expression of both.

Projection, if it doesn't go as far as identification, is actually quite useful. When we assume that some quality or characteristic is present in another, and then, through experience, find that this is not true, we are obliged to realize that the world is not our own creation. If we are reflective, we can learn something about ourselves. This is called withdrawing projections. It isn't easy, and it doesn't happen overnight, but it is part and parcel of growing up.

It only becomes necessary to withdraw projections when our expectations of others are frustrated. If there is no obvious disparity between what we expect, or imagine to be true, and the reality the other faces us with, there is no need to withdraw projections. Don't look a gift horse in the mouth; let sleeping dogs lie—as long as they do.

Also on the positive side, it must be said that projection can constellate unrealized or dormant qualities in another person. Parental expectations notoriously lead one astray, but they can also be the stimulus to explore one's potential. Many a grown woman has achieved more than she might have without a friend's injunction: "You can do it!" And many a man owes his accomplishments to similar urgings from a loved one behind the throne. As long as power over the other, or one's own unlived life, is not lurking in the shadows, such projections do no harm at all.

So much for the dynamics of projection. There is more that can be said, but not without repeating myself more than I already have.[2]

*

Meanwhile, out of rehab and back at the ranch, I was getting used to being home again and cooking things I actually liked to eat: rib eye steaks, pork chops, sausages, spare ribs, pepperoni pizza and the like. Well, fatty

---

[2] See my book *Jungian Psychology Unplugged: My Life As an Elephant,* pp. 59ff.

protein, yum yum, reportedly healthy for O-positive blood types like me. (Of course I paid particular attention to turning the stove off after cooking). I had regular blood tests that showed my cholesterol was okay and iron levels too. Also, the rehab folks had arranged for what they called community care, so for six weeks an occupational therapist, code-name Jennifer, came to me on Tuesdays at 5:30 for an hour.

Dear Jenny was young and perky, cute as a button, and we hit it off right away. There was no hanky-panky, for that was ethically proscribed (her call, not mine you can be sure). So we talked and played O.T. games with cards and puzzles and Ms. Button massaged me with sweet talk about how well I was doing for an old duffer who had been through a major physical trauma and still dreamed of tripping over IV lines. Ah, we had a great time skirting our mutual attraction, or so it seemed at the time thanks to my projection.

Well, I took her findings to heart. Although the surgery and stroke were by this time only distant memories, I was beginning to appreciate the fact that I might have died or been seriously incapacitated, and also that I was truly loved by more than a few—witness a stack of "get well" cards a foot high and the many phone calls from those who had heard of my situation.

I had taken my life somewhat for granted. Now I savored anew what I had and those who were along for the journey. I developed a new appreciation of my mortality and how to enjoy it. Every night I fell asleep feeling blessed and awoke the next day ditto, come rain or come shine. Then I went about doing what was right in front of me, as always.

2
On the Path

I am often asked by those who work with me analytically, "What should I do? What is my rightful path?" Another common question is: "Am I getting anywhere, am I making progress?"

These are tough questions to answer. They might as well ask, "Am I pregnant?"—for I am obliged to reply: "How would I know?"

It's the father complex, you see, making you think that someone knows you better than you know yourself, not to mention the ubiquitous illusion that there is something or somewhere to get or progress to. . . .

Let me take you behind the scenes of a typical analytic session, including something of what goes on in me. I say "typical," but in fact every session is different, even with the same person. But at least I can impart the flavor of the so-called analytic encounter as I have experienced it.[3]

Norman plonked himself down on the sofa. Glum, glum. His mood was like a fog between us.

"The world is a turd," he said.

"A turd?" I repeated. Perhaps he had some mythological concept in mind. I knew that among some Indian tribes in South America human excrement was consecrated to the gods.

"Living alone is the shits," he said, tears in his eyes. "I can't do it, I have to go back."

At this point Norman had been away from his wife and three kids for several months. He was living in a basement apartment in a run-down part of Toronto. He had one small room and a kitchenette and a bathroom. Every Saturday morning he went to visit his family in their country home. He played with the kids, helped with the shopping, did a few

---

[3] Some of the material in this chapter first appeared in my earlier work, *The Survival Papers: Anatomy of a Midlife Crisis.* For another persepctive, see Mario Jacoby, *The Analytic Encounter.*

odd jobs. On Sunday evening he returned to his cell in the city.

Norman's situation was familiar to me. It was much the same as that of many dislocated fathers. And mothers too. In fact it was a Jamaican lady who first pointed out to me: "You lives alone, you pays your dues. You lives with your family, you pays your dues. Either way you pays dues. You makes your choice and you lives with it best you can. Amen, praise the Lord, hallelujah."

I can't say better than that.

"I left," said Norman, "because it seemed to me the only way I had a chance to live, Now I'm not so sure. What if I made the wrong decision? What if it's just an easy way out of my real responsibilities?"

"Apparently not so easy at that," I grimaced.

"I feel skewered between my anima and my mother complex," he went on. "My anima won't let me live with Nancy, and my mother complex won't let me live without her."

Norman had picked up the jargon. I wasn't happy about that, but you can't stop people from reading.

* "I tried to make love to Nancy when I was home last weekend," he said. "She did her usual stone act and I couldn't get it up. God, I'm so frustrated!"

The tears welled up. "It's a half-life," he said bitterly. "It's almost worse than nothing at all."

Norman took out a handkerchief and blew his nose. He said:

On Saturday night I dreamed of Eleanor. (Remember her? We had a thing for a few days last year in Des Moines.) In the dream she came to visit Nancy and me. I took her down to the basement and explained the situation. The light was very dim. It was like we were in a mineshaft. As Eleanor left, I called out to her, "I'm talking to you from the end of a long tunnel!" She was appalled.

I said nothing. I thought Norman was right where he should be. He had a conflict, and only by holding the tension between opposites (more about this later) could he hope to become a free man. For the time being, the opposites were living with his family and living alone.

"When I left Sunday night, Nancy put it to me. 'Either come back to stay or don't come back at all,' she said. "It's too hard on me, and the kids can't stand it either.' "

Norman looked out the window. "Nancy says I have no feeling for her. She needs to have men friends, she says. I agree, and then I feel worse! God, I can't stand her suffering! She acts so strong and I know she isn't. Half the time she's crying when I go home. I'm no help to her, I feel like a child. How can I get her to love me?"

My heart went out to Norman but my tongue was tied. I had very little to offer—no solutions, no pat answers. He was a victim of his own psychology, no more, no less. His past was a memory, his present a shambles. After a year of analysis he had a better understanding of himself, but his future was unknown. The ball was in his court: How to be a man?

"Look at it this way," I said, "You have an opportunity to grow up. If your wife were passionately interested in you, you might still be unconscious. It's like when Eve ate the apple and she and Adam were thrown out of the Garden. According to the Church it was a *felix culpa,* a fortunate crime, the beginning of the history of consciousness. You can't become conscious if you stay in the Garden."

"You mean I'm conscious now?" asked Norman, fishing.

"I was speaking about your potential," I said.

He lapsed into silence.

Me too, as I am thinking: Consciousness is not a one-time thing, it's an on-going struggle. It's like treading water for a lifetime. Sometimes you go under. If you keep your wits about you, you bob back up. If you don't, you sink into the depths.

I believe that Norman's fate is largely dependent on unconscious factors. More: the unconscious is Janus-faced: on the one hand its contents point back to a preconscious, prehistoric world of instinct, while on the other it anticipates the future, even shows the way to it. It is the task of consciousness to endure the open conflict that often exists between the two. It's the old game of hammer and anvil. Between them, in the tension, the individual is forged.

The unconscious is too big to beat, and falling into it is to give up the struggle entirely. What is left? You can take a stand toward it. That is called becoming conscious.

"What do you want?" I asked Norman.

He looked bleak. "It's not a question of what I want. More like what I can stand. I have a horror of growing old all alone. I have gray pubic hairs. That's disgusting! I think of being an old man in a hospital bed, near the end, and no one comes to say good-by. Nobody loves me! I'm on my own!"

The tears broke through. He fell back and sobbed.

Poor baby. I passed the box of Kleenex and recalled more of my own past.

I was in analysis for about two months before I cried in front of my analyst. Whatever happened outside, in my analytic hours I was determined to be a stand-up guy. I wanted to impress my analyst; I wanted him to like and respect me. I had an urbane persona to live up to, my image of myself. I would not willingly drop it in front of my analyst. He was the person in whose eyes I most wanted to shine. And so, I seldom told him how I really felt about anything. I feared he would judge me as weak.

This charade came to an end the day my analyst's comments struck a nerve that was so raw my defenses failed. At the time I thought it was quite accidental. Today, having pushed a few buttons myself, I'm not so sure.

I remember it well. It was a bright Thursday morning. That is not normal in Zurich. While the surrounding mountains may be bathed in sunshine, the city itself is invariably overcast and gray. Meteorologically, Zurich invites depression. The weather reports speak of highs and lows, and that's just the way it was for me.

My analyst's office was lined with bookshelves. Personal mementos were everywhere. Flowers too. I loved that place. Once a week I sat there for an hour and felt safe.

"How have you been?" he would ask.

"Good; really, really good," I would lie.

Should I tell him about my crying in the night? Should I tell him how lonely I was, how I felt about my housemate Arnold's interm-inable parties? Would he be interested to know that I got into bed with two women one night and couldn't get an erection? What would he think if I told him I was afraid of dogs? How would he react to my prowling the bars along the Niederdorf? Should I tell him about my experiments with dope? About the woman who bit me in a pub?

I forced a smile. "Nothing special."

He fell silent, as he usually did, waiting for me to say what was on my mind.

I read from my journal, my usual routine. I had diligently recorded each day's events—edited to make me look good—followed by the dreams each night and my associations to their bizarre images. I amplified the themes from mythology and religion and reflected at length on their psychological meaning.

No doubt about it, I was really a prize student. I did everything I was supposed to. I could not be faulted on procedure.

"And what else?" asked my analyst, smoothing the top of his head where no hair grew.

"What else what?" I said, looking up.

"What else occurs to you," he said. "What else do you think of, about this woman in your dream, this unknown female who asks you for a dance?"

"Well, she's my anima, isn't she?"

"I don't speak Greek," said my analyst. "Explain, please."

I leaned back, confident. "The anima is my inner woman," I said. "Everybody knows that. Apparently she wants to get closer to me." I laughed. "I have no objection."

My analyst leaned forward. "That's bullshit," he said.

I cringed. Tears stung my eyes. I opened my mouth to speak and nothing came out. For a few minutes I cried uncontrollably. I also had the hiccups.

I wiped my face. "Sorry about that," I said. "I don't know what came over me."

My analyst looked quite stern. His eyes were slightly in shadow from the reading lamp between us. He clasped and unclasped his hands. I felt naked, stripped to the bone. I hung there, expecting to be banished. My eyes took in his books, his antique desk, the lush green plants, an upright piano in one corner, and the window looking to the lake. I fastened on his bald spot, waiting. Please, God, I thought, do not tell me I'm unworthy.

Then he smiled, openly, a rare breaking of the lips that to me sang of acceptance. He rubbed his hands. "Now we do analysis," he said, "if that's what you want."

That was about thirty years ago. But I still remember that session, and many others, because they were turning points. On that Thursday morning I developed a degree of trust for my analyst that hadn't been there before. I broke down and it was okay.

In this respect Norman had the jump on me. The first time he came he cried the whole hour. He never put on a false front. His emotions were always close to the surface and he didn't try to hide them.

"I went to a party last night," Norman was saying. "There were plenty of girls, but I had no appetite. About midnight I phoned Nancy. She was curt; I'd woken her up. I cried for five minutes. I really wanted to go home.

"Nancy was not happy about that. 'I don't like you like this,' she said, 'I wish you'd work it out.' She finally hung up on me.

"Work it out! Je-suz! What if I can't? What if this is my life?"

I shrugged.

"I'm so ambivalent," said Norman. "Whatever way I turn in my head—to be with her or not—seems right for a few minutes, then it flips. When Nancy is cold, I think I can't go back, I would die there. But all she has to do is smile or touch me, or look at me like she used to, and those thoughts are out the window. Well yes, I think, I can live with her after all. And then she makes a stinging comment and I'm back in the soup. Woe is me!"

I'm thinking: woe is *we,* for I am no stranger to being in the soup, and ambivalence is my second home. It doesn't always involve women but it invariably goes hand in hand with conflict.

One of the lengthiest conflicts I ever endured was over a job offer from a publisher I'd been working for while I was training in Zurich. It was a large publishing operation, very classy books. They wanted me to take over as editor-in-chief. I was flattered. The salary was more than generous and it would be interesting work. But I still had a year to go to finish my analytic training.

I talked it over with my analyst. "I don't think I want the job but I can't bring myself to turn it down. What should I do?"

"I don't know," he shrugged.

"Maybe I won't like being an analyst," I fretted. "Don't you ever get bored, listening to people's problems all day?"

"Sometimes it's hard to stay awake." He smiled. "But it keeps me in touch with myself."

My housemate Arnold said: "Sure, it's a great opportunity. But think about why we came here in the first place."

At that time Arnold was washing dishes in a posh Zurich café. It was black work; he didn't have a permit. The pay wasn't good but he brought home lots of cold cuts.

Rachel, my inner woman, was elusive in those days; she had nothing meaningful to say.

I went back and forth in my mind for several weeks. The tension was awful. I could not decide.

I finally told the publisher I would accept the job if he added a secretary and I could arrange my schedule to continue my studies at the Jung Institute. He agreed.

"You're bonkers," said Arnold, "you can't do both."

I panicked. I asked for more money and a travel allowance. The publisher talked to his higher-ups and got the okay.

Now I was really terrified.

"What am I going to do?" I said to my analyst. "Every time I up the ante he agrees!"

He smiled. "You seem to want him to make your decision. Apparently he knows what he wants. Do you?"

That floored me. But finally, after two months of sitting on the fence I rejected the job. The publisher was disappointed. He said only, "I hope you know what you're doing."

At our next session I told my analyst. I thought he'd be proud of me. After all, I'd resisted Mammon.

"Like Christ in the desert," I said, "I stood firm."

He smiled: "An interesting image, but you might have made a better editor than an analyst."

Talk about deflation.

That reconstellated the whole conflict. Had I made the right decision but for the wrong reasons? The wrong decision for the right reasons? Now the opposite came back to haunt me. By then the job had gone to someone else, but the conflict didn't die until Arnold threw a party marking my fortieth birthday.

"Look at me!" he said, shuffling along the floor like José Ferrer playing Toulouse Lautrec. "We have nothing to lose but our knees!"

And get this: that publisher went bankrupt a year later . . .

Norman was staring at me. "You're quiet. You don't say much. Where am I in this process?" he said impatiently. "I watch myself. I write. I paint. Why do I still feel so bad? Am I doing the right thing? You don't tell me. I spill my guts and you hardly speak at all. Dammit! I'm not even sure you're listening."

I'd heard that before. It used to unnerve me.

"What is it you want to hear?" I said.

"I don't know," replied Norman. "You're the expert."

I shook my head. "No."

"You are!" he insisted. "You've been trained. You know the mysteries, I don't. Tell me what is true. Wipe the scales from my eyes. Show me the light!"

I polished my half-glasses with a tissue, wondering if my Japanese maple would survive the frost. I was not indifferent to Norman's plight, but he had some expectations I couldn't meet. Call it projection, call it transference, he saw me as his savior. It wasn't his fault, that's just the way it is. You invest other people with your own potential. And when they don't live up to it, you get testy.

"I know some theories and I have experienced my own process," I said to Norman. "That's all. Your behavior and your problems fit some patterns I'm familiar with, but you yourself are unique. I can't plumb your depths. That's up to you if you have the heart for it. Be patient. A solution to your life, a way out of the maze, will crystallize in you."

In my head I was hearing my Zurich analyst saying something similar. Like Norman I had been frustrated without explicit guidance. I believed my analyst held the key to my life, all those locked doors. It was perverse of him to let me stew.

"Release me," I begged one day.

It was some months after my crying jag. I'd had a particularly difficult week. Money was low, my teeth hurt and my girlfriend thought she was pregnant. And Arnold kept me awake at night practicing on his banjo.

"You *know* me," I said to my analyst, "you can do it."

I clammed up. Already this much, with its implied criticism, took all my courage.

My analyst was not one to make speeches. On that occasion, however, he did not mince words.

"You misunderstand this process," he said. "It's all in your hands. Think of what you have been, what you are and what you could be. Reflect on your material, pay close attention to what happens in your life and talk to me about it. I will listen and from time to time I will respond. If I'm silent it's because I have nothing to say.

"You pay for my time and my integrity. I have questions but no answers, no secret prescription. I focus on your process only during our hours together. Outside of analysis I attend to my own life. If you expect more, you will be disappointed. Look on me simply as one of your tools."

You made that up, said Rachel. Be quiet, I said, it's close enough.

I smiled at Norman.

"It's not fair!" he said with some heat. "You know things you won't tell me."

I thought a minute. What I knew for sure I could put in a teacup. And it would still be mostly dregs. To Norman I said:

"It's true I could say more than I do. The question is whether it would make any difference. Do you think there is nothing going on between us except what we say to each other? Do you think that's all there is?"

Norman blushed. He had had ample evidence over the past year that the unconscious had a say in everything.

"Healing, if it takes place at all," I said, "has little to do with conscious intentions. You imagine I can heal your wounds. You forget your own inner healer and my wounds."

I picked up volume 16 of Jung's Collected Works. "Here," I said, "go home and read this essay, 'The Psychology of the Transference.'

"Now, let's get back to work. Tell me all your associations to this woman in your dream . . . Eleanor?"

Thank goodness Norman had dreams. I am quite lost without these nightly commentaries on one's daily life and attitudes. I may not understand what they mean, but in analytic work they are a good place to start, and without them there are only opinions.

That's the major difference between analysis and therapy. Therapy is generally supportive; it focuses on building up ego strength. Analysis is a process that is only appropriate—or even possible—with an already well-developed ego (albeit one that may be in a crisis). Therapy tends toward ironing out one's wrinkles in adapting to collective life. Analysis is an open-ended discipline that aims to collaborate with one's potential, and in this pursuit it depends on messages from the unconscious—and particularly dreams—to balance conscious attitudes that may be out of whack with a person's overall personality.

*

When Norman left, I thought of the possibility that he was not cut out for analysis, that he might kill himself. It had come up before. In the past, his mildly suicidal thoughts had evaporated as his natural enthusiasm for life took over. I had to trust in that. Suicide is a real option only for those who have no hope. Norman was depressed, but to my mind far from hopeless. He'd tough it out.

Alone that night, I reread Jung's essay, the one I'd recommended to Norman. I had almost forgotten how very good it is. It's all there, the alpha and omega of the analytic process.

When I first entered analysis it was just another course to me, like being at university. The goal was grades. You did your best and you passed or failed.

This is not what happens in analysis. Here your best is not what you have to offer intellectually, nor is your worst. The goal is individuation—becoming who you were meant to be—but even that, Jung points out, "is important only as an idea; the essential thing is the opus"—the work on yourself— "which leads to the goal; that is the goal of a lifetime."[4]

Moreover, you are graded, if at all—and even then not by your analyst—on what is in your heart.

There are a lot of dull hours in analysis when nothing seems to be happening. There is the occasional Eureka! But sometimes change takes years. The revelations, the insights, come only after prolonged attention to the mundane. This is quite a shock to those who go into analysis seeking the divine. Of course, the psyche is full of mystery—as is the work of analysis—so perhaps there is a divine element in both.

People have come to me because they wanted to understand their visions. When they realize there is nothing special about having visions, that they're as common as turnips and that their task is to come down to earth, they often stop analysis.

People come to me because they *want* to have visions. I send them away. I have a great respect for visions, but I don't know how to create them.

I've seen others who thought analysis would make them gods, invulnerable. They stopped because it doesn't. And then there are some who go into analysis just because they think it's a good idea. They don't last long either, there's no edge. And of course there are those who stop out of sheer frustration; they can't make the connection between what goes on at night, in their dreams, and everyday life.

Daily life is the raw material of analysis. It's analogous to what the alchemists called the *prima materia*—lead, the base metal they strived to

---

[4] "The Psychology of the Transference," *The Practice of Psychotherapy.* CW 16, par. 400. [CW refers throughout to *The Collected Works of C.G. Jung.*]

turn into gold. Psychologically this refers to one's moods and dreams, attitudes, feelings, thoughts. And especially the nitty-gritty detail, the "he said" and "she said" encounters that bring you to a boil but you'd like to forget when you cool down.

All this you write down in a journal. That takes some discipline, but if you don't keep a journal, you don't remember.

Of course you can't record everything. You'd get lost in the forest and miss the trees. You note the highlights, particularly emotional reactions—because they signal the presence of complexes—and your conscious attitude toward them. You mull all this over and you take your reflections to your analyst.

Time is a big factor in this process. An hour or two a week is never enough, but when it's all you've got you soon get used to it. The real work in any case is what you do between sessions, on your own, or not; and if not, then little of a transformative nature happens.

I think of the poet Rilke's story of his neighbor, a Russian bureaucrat named Nikolai Kusmitch.

Time was precious to Nikolai Kusmitch. He spent his days hoarding it, saving a second here, a minute or two there, sometimes a whole half hour. He imagined that the time he saved could be used to better advantage when he wasn't so busy. Perhaps it could even be tacked on at the end of his life, so he'd live longer.

He sought out what he thought must exist, a state institution for time, a kind of Time Bank you could make deposits in and then draw on. He didn't find one, so he kept the loose change in his head.

Nikolai Kusmitch did what he could to economize, but after a few weeks it struck him that he was still spending too much.

"I must retrench," he thought.

He rose earlier. He washed less thoroughly, ate his toast standing up and drank coffee on the run. But on Sundays, when he came to settle his accounts, he always found that nothing remained of his savings. He died as he had lived, a pauper.[5]

---

[5] Rainer Maria Rilke, *The Notebooks of Malte Laurids Brigge*, pp. 16ff, paraphrase.

Working on yourself is something like that. You can't save it up for Sundays; it's what you do during the week that counts.

*

Jung described complexes as islands of consciousness, split off from the ego-mainland. It's a useful metaphor. When you're emotional, caught in a complex, you're cut off from rational ego resources; the complex rules the personality as long as you stay on the island. When the storm dies down you swim back to the mainland and lick your wounds, wondering what got into you.

When you occupy an island most of the time—as Norman does, living on the mother, so to speak—a "monster" is constellated in the surrounding waters, the unconscious. Curiously enough, that creature is one's potential salvation. Jung describes it like this:

> The island is a bit cramped and . . . life on it is pretty meagre and plagued with all sorts of imaginary wants because too much life has been left outside. As a result a terrifying monster is created, or rather is roused out of its slumbers. . . . This seemingly alarming animal stands in a secret compensatory relationship to the island and could supply everything that the island lacks.[6]

One might think the ego has what the island lacks. Alas, it doesn't. If it did, the island would not have formed in the first place. Islands are after all only refuges for what is unacceptable to those living on the mainland. The mainland in this context is not so much an ego as a persona, which would like to rid itself of anything unconventional.

I see, said Rachel, like England sending its convicted criminals to Australia. Tsk, tsk, I said, that's just one island dumping its garbage on another.

A human personality is made up of an ego and any number of island complexes. The task in analysis is to establish a beachhead on the ego-mainland that is a more satisfactory living space than any of the islands,

---

[6] "The Psychology of the Transference," *The Practice of Psychotherapy*, CW 16, par. 374.

and at the same time make friends with the animals, the instincts, in the unconscious. That is what can happen, through projection, in the analytic relationship.

As a general rule the unconscious first appears in projected form. In analysis this is called transference: the analysand's beachhead, the still unconscious healing "answer," is projected onto the analyst, whose response is called the countertransference. It's a set-up. The analyst knows both that he is expected to heal and that he cannot. Nevertheless, he can be tricked into believing it is possible.

The transference is as many-headed as the mythical Hydra and has as many arms as an octopus. The analyst parries its blows while awaiting the constellation of the healing factor in the analysand.

How this happens, if and when it does, has given rise to speculation about a wounded healer archetype, a dynamic presumed to be at work in a therapeutic relationship. The name derives from the legend of Asclepius, a famous Greek doctor who in recognition of his own wounds set up a sanctuary where others could come to be healed of theirs.

Those seeking to be cured went through a process called incubation. First they had a cleansing bath. This was thought to have a purifying effect on the soul as well as the body. After some preliminary sacrificial offerings, the incubants lay on a couch—Greek *cline*, whence derives the name for our modern clinics—and went to sleep. If they were lucky, they had a healing dream and woke up feeling great. If they were even luckier, a snake came in the night and bit them.[7]

The use of a couch in classical Freudian analysis stems from this ancient practice. Few Jungians use a couch, preferring to sit face to face, but it sometimes appears symbolically in the preamble to dreams ("I am lying on a couch . . .") to indicate that the unconscious has been activated.

The wounded healer archetype can be schematized by the same "cross-cousin marriage" diagram used by Jung to illustrate the many

---

[7] See C.A. Meier, *Ancient Incubation and Modern Psychotherapy.*

lines of communication in any relationship.[8] Only the labels are different.

The drawing below shows six double-headed arrows, indicating that communication moves in both directions. That makes twelve ways in which information can pass between analyst and analysand.

According to this paradigm, although the analyst is presumed to have become somewhat conscious of his or her own wounds—through a lengthy personal analysis—they still live a shadowy existence. Which is to say, they don't hurt so much, but they can always be reconstellated by phantoms from the past or by contact with someone whose wounds are similar.

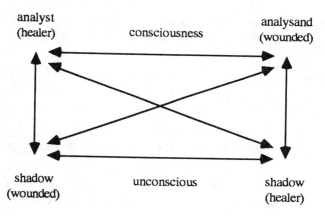

Enter the analysand on his knees, hurting but not knowing why. His inner healer is in his shadow, potentially available. Various dialogues take place, one at a time or simultaneously, as shown by the diagram. The analysand's wounds are transferred through the unconscious onto the analyst, who experiences, say, a headache or a knot in the stomach. The analyst reacts to this, identifies the wounds and attempts to reach a conscious understanding of them. In one way or another the analyst's awareness is passed back to the analysand.

---

[8] See "The Psychology of the Transference," *The Practice of Psychotherapy,* CW 16, par. 422.

That's what's supposed to happen, and sometimes it does. But it might take years. In this model, the unconscious relationship between analyst and analysand is quite as important, in terms of the healing process,[9] as what is actually said—and perhaps even more so. As James Hillman points out:

> In an analysis, the intimacy grows between two people less through the horizontal connection than through the parallel vertical connections of each within himself. Each listens as much to the effect of the other within and to these inner reactions as to the other. Each takes the other in.[10]

The implications of all this are twofold:

1) Healing can take place only if the analyst has an ongoing relationship with the unconscious, that is, stays aware of his shadowy wounds. Otherwise he identifies with the healer—a form of inflation—and they're both in the soup.

2) Depth psychology is a dangerous profession. An analyst is ever prone to being infected by the other's wounds. This happens when you take on somebody else's problems as if they were your own. There's a thin line between empathy and identification, hence the high incidence of depression and even suicide among those in the so-called helping professions.

It is now well known that analysis is not a panacea, that some people do not "improve" or "get better," no matter how much analysis they have. The mystery is what happens when it works, why some people actually benefit from it. The wounded healer concept makes sense to me.

*

Norman has been at this for over a year. He came for the right reason—he had nowhere else to go. He knows in his head that analysis is open-ended; it's not like going to a doctor for a quick fix, a pill to kill the pain. However, he'd still like to get it over with, be "cured." He doesn't

---

[9] See C. Jess Groesbeck, "The Archetypal Image of the Wounded Healer," in *Journal of Analytical Psychology*, vol. 20, no. 2 (July 1975), pp. 122ff.

[10] *Insearch*, p. 38. Of course, the same may be said of what goes on between two people in any heartfelt relationship: "Each takes the other in."

yet realize that it will never be over, that he'll always be up against himself.

Well, that's the long and the short of being "on the path." And good luck to you.

3
Inner Others

The core of the Jungian approach to mental health is that the psyche is self-regulating; that is, it will balance itself over time. Of course, it may stall in this task—often in midlife—and then it might need a little nudge, like paying extra-close attention to what is happening in your life, keeping a journal, identifying your inner companions and then dialoguing with them. Such are the necessary activities if one is serious in pursuing what Jung called the process of individuation.

When I was a young man, I was concerned to figure out where and how I might fit into the larger picture, how to make a mark. I had a fantasy that somewhere there was a big book of collective wisdom that contained prescribed solutions to all life's problems. Whenever you found yourself in a quandary you could just look it up in *The Big Book* and do what it said. (In my mind's eye it had a really good index, too.) Such a fantasy is symptomatic of an active father complex. If there were such a book, I wouldn't have to think for myself. I'd just do what was laid down by tradition.

More about this later. For now I will just say that to my mind there are no "detours" in life. Your path is what you are living, be it ever so joyful or not so. Do what is next, right in front of you, and I think you will not go astray. Don't fret over making "mistakes" or wrong choices. There is only what you do because you are who you are, and so you can do no other. It is what the Greeks called *moira,* fate. That is what in Jung-speak we call the process of individuation. In later years—when you stop feeling you have to prove yourself, say, and have time to reflect—you may look back and discern the pattern that is you—your fate. Jung said as much after a heart attack that almost ended his life:

> When one follows the path of individuation, when one lives one's own life, one must take mistakes into the bargain; life would not be complete without them. There is no guarantee—not for a single moment—that we

will not fall into error or stumble into deadly peril. We may think there is a sure road. But that would be the road of death. Then nothing happens any longer—at any rate, not the right things. Anyone who takes the sure road is as good as dead.[11]

I think of those many fairy tales of three brothers who set out to win their father's approval: one goes east and ends up in the whore's cellar; one goes west and falls into a deep abyss; while the third and youngest—the so-called Dummling—goes straight ahead and finds the princess who weaves garments with a golden thread and is herself "the treasure hard to attain."

In Jung-speak, a man's inner princess is called the anima—his feminine side, his soul and access to eros (as opposed to logos, presumably his more natural habitat). The anima tells a man how he feels. She is also a kind of psychopomp who mediates the unconscious to ego-consciousness, and is therefore inherently his creative muse.

I could not have written any of my books without the help of my anima. I have often code-named her Rachel, but I might just as well have called her Beatrice (as Dante did) or Aphrodite (as the Greeks did), or Nurse Pam or Godzilla; no matter, by any name she was and is my muse. And incidentally, curiously, at any age she is mostly a perfect size 34-b, as if that made a difference to anyone except models and couturiers. More: I could not have survived at all without a lively, ongoing relationship with her, whether she manifested inside or out. You see, a man without a relationship to his inner feminine is a man without a soul. He will physically and emotionally abuse women. And God help his lady friends if he is also a religious fundamentalist.

Adam was pacing, eager to put his oar in. "The anima," he noted, "is both a personal complex and an archetypal image of woman in the male psyche. It is an unconscious factor incarnated anew in every male child, and is responsible for the mechanism of projection. Initially identified with the personal mother, the anima is later experienced not only in other women but as a pervasive influence in a man's life."

---

[11] *Memories, Dreams, Reflections,* p. 297.

Okay, moving right along, here are some things Jung has to say about a man's inner feminine side:

The anima is the *archetype of life itself.*[12]

There is [in man] an imago not only of the mother but of the daughter, the sister, the beloved, the heavenly goddess, and the chthonic Baubo. Every mother and every beloved is forced to become the carrier and embodiment of this omnipresent and ageless image, which corresponds to the deepest reality in a man. It belongs to him, this perilous image of Woman; she stands for the loyalty which in the interests of life he must sometimes forego; she is the much needed compensation for the risks, struggles, sacrifices that all end in disappointment; she is the solace for all the bitterness of life. And, at the same time, she is the great illusionist, the seductress, who draws him into life with her Maya—and not only into life's reasonable and useful aspects, but into its frightful paradoxes and ambivalences where good and evil, success and ruin, hope and despair, counterbalance one another. Because she is his greatest danger she demands from a man his greatest, and if he has it in him she will receive it.[13]

The anima is personified in dreams by images of women ranging from seductress to spiritual guide. She is associated with the eros principle; hence a man's anima development is reflected in how he relates to actual women. Within his own psyche, the anima functions as his soul, influencing his ideas, attitudes and emotions.

The anima is not the soul in the dogmatic sense, not an *anima rationalis,* which is a philosophical conception, but a natural archetype that satisfactorily sums up all the statements of the unconscious, of the primitive mind, of the history of language and religion. . . . It is always the *a priori* element in [a man's] moods, reactions, impulses, and whatever else is spontaneous in psychic life.[14]

---

12 "Archetypes of the Collective Unconscious," *The Archetypes and the Collective Unconscious,* CW 9i, par. 66.

13 "The Syzygy: Anima and Animus," *Aion,* CW 9ii, par. 24

14 "Archetypes of the Collective Unconscious," *The Archetypes and the Collective Unconscious,* CW 9i, par. 57.

The anima . . . intensifies, exaggerates, falsifies, and mythologizes all emotional relations with [a man's] work and with other people of both sexes. The resultant fantasies and entanglements are all her doing. When the anima is strongly constellated, she softens the man's character and makes him touchy, irritable, moody, jealous, vain, and unadjusted.[15]

As an inner personality, the anima is complementary to the persona and stands in a compensatory relationship to it.

The persona, the ideal picture of a man as he should be, is inwardly compensated by feminine weakness, and as the individual outwardly plays the strong man, so he becomes inwardly a woman, i.e., the anima, for it is the anima that reacts to the persona. But because the inner world is dark and invisible . . . and because a man is all the less capable of conceiving his weaknesses the more he is identified with the persona, the persona's counterpart, the anima, remains completely in the dark and is at once projected, so that our hero comes under the heel of his wife's slipper.[16]

Hence the character of the anima can generally be deduced from that of the persona; all those qualities absent from the outer attitude will be found in the inner:

The tyrant tormented by bad dreams, gloomy forebodings, and inner fears is a typical figure. Outwardly ruthless, harsh, and unapproachable, he jumps inwardly at every shadow, is at the mercy of every mood, as though he were the feeblest and most impressionable of men. Thus his anima contains all those fallible human qualities his persona lacks. If the persona is intellectual, the anima will certainly be sentimental.[17]

Similarly, where a man identifies with his persona, he is in effect possessed by the anima, with attendant symptoms. Here is how Jung puts it:

Identity with the persona automatically leads to an unconscious identity with the anima because, when the ego is not differentiated from the persona, it can have no conscious relation to the unconscious processes. Consequently it *is* these processes, it is identical with them. Anyone who is

---

[15] "Concerning the Archetypes and the Anima Concept," ibid., par. 144.

[16] "Anima and Animus," *Two Essays on Analytical Psychology,* CW 7, par. 309.

[17] "Definitions," *Psychological Types,* CW 6, par. 804.

himself his outward role will infallibly succumb to the inner processes; he will either frustrate his outward role by absolute inner necessity or else reduce it to absurdity, by a process of enantiodromia. Moreover, the anima is inevitably projected upon a real object, with which he gets into a relation of almost total dependence.[18]

Jung distinguished four broad stages of the anima, analogous to levels of the Eros cult in the late classical period. He personified them as Eve, Helen, Mary and Sophia.[19]

The first stage, Eve, is purely biological; woman is equated with the mother and only represents something to be fertilized. In the second stage, personified in the historical figure of Helen of Troy, the anima is a collective and ideal sexual image that as an outer woman can enthrall a man. In the third stage, Mary as the personification of Christian devotion manifests in religious feelings and a capacity for lasting relationships. In the fourth stage, as Sophia (called Wisdom in the Bible), a man's anima functions as a guide to the inner life, mediating to consciousness the contents of the unconscious. She cooperates in the search for meaning and is the creative muse in a man's life.

Ideally, a man's anima proceeds naturally through these stages as he grows older. In fact, as an archetypal life force, the anima manifests in whatever shape or form is necessary to compensate the dominant conscious attitude. For instance, if a man becomes too cerebral and alienated from the "baser" instincts, his anima might entice him into pubs or strip joints—just to show him who's boss.

Adam stepped in here: "So long as the anima is unconscious, everything she stands for is projected. Most commonly, because of the initially close tie between the anima and the protective mother-imago, this projection falls on a man's partner, with predictable results." He then quoted remarks from Jung:

> [A man's] ideal of marriage is so arranged that his wife has to take over the magical role of the mother. Under the cloak of the ideally exclusive

---

[18] Ibid., par. 807.

[19] "The Psychology of the Transference," *The Practice of Psychotherapy,* CW 16, par. 361.

marriage he is really seeking his mother's protection, and thus he plays into the hands of his wife's possessive instincts. His fear of the dark incalculable power of the unconscious gives his wife an illegitimate authority over him, and forges such a dangerously close union that the marriage is permanently on the brink of explosion from internal tension.[20]

No matter where a man is in terms of psychological development, he is always prone to see aspects of his anima, his soul, in an outer woman. The same is true of the animus, a woman's inner man. Their personal aspects may be integrated and their significance understood, but their essential nature cannot be exhausted.

Though the effects of anima and animus can be made conscious, they themselves are factors transcending consciousness and beyond the reach of perception and volition. Hence they remain autonomous despite the integration of their contents, and for this reason they should be borne constantly in mind.[21]

The psychological priority in the first half of life is for a man to free himself from the anima fascination of the mother. In later life, the lack of a conscious relationship with the anima is attended by symptoms characteristic of what so-called primitives knew as "loss of soul." Jung again:

Younger people . . . can bear even the total loss of the anima without injury. The important thing at this stage is for a man to be a man. . . .
After the middle of life, however, permanent loss of the anima means a diminution of vitality, of flexibility, and of human kindness. The result, as a rule, is premature rigidity, crustiness, stereotypy, fanatical one-sidedness, obstinacy, pedantry, or else resignation, weariness, sloppiness, irresponsibility, and finally a childish *ramollissement* [petulance] with a tendency to alcohol.[22]

One way for a man to become familiar with the nature of his anima is through the method of active imagination. This is done by personifying

---

[20] "Anima and Animus," *Two Essays on Analytical Psychology*, CW 7, par. 316.
[21] "The Syzygy: Anima and Animus," *Aion*, CW 9ii, par. 40.
[22] "Concerning the Archetypes and the Anima Concept," *The Archetypes and the Collective Unconscious*, CW 9i, par. 146f.

her as an autonomous personality, asking her questions and attending to the response. Writes Jung:

> I mean this as an actual technique. . . . The art of it consists only in allowing our invisible partner to make herself heard, in putting the mechanism of expression momentarily at her disposal, without being overcome by the distaste one naturally feels at playing such an apparently ludicrous game with oneself, or by doubts as to the genuineness of the voice of one's interlocutor.[23]

Jung suggested that if the encounter with the shadow is the "apprentice-piece" in a man's psychological development, then coming to terms with the anima is the "master-piece."[24] The goal is the transformation of the anima from a troublesome adversary into a function of relationship between consciousness and the unconscious. Jung called this "the conquest of the anima as an autonomous complex."

> With the attainment of this goal it becomes possible to disengage the ego from all its entanglements with collectivity and the collective unconscious. Through this process the anima forfeits the daemonic power of an autonomous complex; she can no longer exercise the power of possession, since she is depotentiated. She is no longer the guardian of treasures unknown; no longer Kundry, daemonic Messenger of the Grail, half divine and half animal; no longer is the soul to be called "Mistress," but a psychological function of an intuitive nature, akin to what the primitives mean when they say, "He has gone into the forest to talk with the spirits" or "My snake spoke with me" or, in the mythological language of infancy, "A little bird told me."[25]

While we're at it, to be fair and for the fun of it, we should attend to the nature of the other contrasexual complex: a woman's animus, her inner masculine side which can be either destructive or life-affirming, depending on her relationship with him. Like the anima in a man, the

---

23 "Anima and Animus," *Two Essays on Analytical Psychology,* CW 7, pars. 323f.

24 "Archetypes of the Collective Unconscious," *The Archetypes and the Collective Unconscious,* CW 9i, par. 61.

25 "The Mana-Personality," *Two Essays on Analytical Psychology,* CW 7, par. 374.

animus is both a personal complex and an archetypal image. Jung writes:

> Woman is compensated by a masculine element and therefore her unconscious has, so to speak, a masculine imprint. This results in a considerable psychological difference between men and women, and accordingly I have called the projection-making factor in women the animus, which means mind or spirit. The animus corresponds to the paternal logos just as the anima corresponds to the maternal eros.[26]

> The animus is the deposit, as it were, of all woman's ancestral experiences of man—and not only that, he is also a creative and procreative being, not in the sense of masculine creativity, but in the sense that he brings forth something we might call the spermatic word.[27]

Whereas the anima in a man functions as his soul, a woman's animus is more like an unconscious mind.[28] It manifests negatively in fixed ideas, collective opinions, and unconscious, *a priori* assumptions that lay claim to absolute truth. In a woman who is identified with the animus (animus-possession in Jung-speak), eros generally takes second place to logos. Jung again:

> A woman possessed by the animus is always in danger of losing her femininity.[29]

> No matter how friendly and obliging a woman's Eros may be, no logic on earth can shake her if she is ridden by the animus. . . . [A man] is unaware that this highly dramatic situation would instantly come to a banal and unexciting end if he were to quit the field and let a second woman carry on the battle (his wife, for instance, if she herself is not the fiery war horse). This sound idea seldom or never occurs to him, because no man can converse with an animus for five minutes without becoming the victim of his own anima.[30]

---

[26] "The Syzygy: Anima and Animus," *Aion,* CW 9ii, pars. 28f.
[27] "Anima and Animus," CW 7, par. 336.
[28] At times Jung also referred to the animus as a woman's soul. See my *Jung Lexicon,* under **soul** and **soul-image.**
[29] "Anima and Animus," CW 7, par. 337.
[30] "The Syzygy: Anima and Animus," *Aion,* CW 9ii, par. 29.

The animus becomes a helpful psychological factor when a woman can tell the difference between the ideas generated by this autonomous complex and what she herself really thinks.

> Like the anima, the animus too has a positive aspect. Through the figure of the father he expresses not only conventional opinion but—equally—what we call "spirit," philosophical or religious ideas in particular, or rather the attitude resulting from them. Thus the animus is a psychopomp, a mediator between the conscious and the unconscious and a personification of the latter.[31]

It is not easy for a woman to discern the difference between herself and her animus, but one clue is that strong emotion always attends the opinions of the negative animus.

Jung described four stages of animus development in a woman, analogous to anima development in a man. He first appears in her life, or in dreams and fantasy, as the embodiment of physical power—an athlete, muscle man or thug. In the second stage, the animus provides her with initiative and the capacity for planned action. He is behind a woman's desire for independence and a career of her own.

In the next stage, the animus is the "word," often personified in dreams as a professor, clergyman, or some other guru. In the fourth stage, the animus is the incarnation of spiritual meaning. On this highest level, like the man's anima as Sophia, the animus mediates between a woman's conscious mind and the unconscious. In mythology this aspect of the animus appears as Hermes, messenger of the gods; in dreams he is a woman's helpful guide to her creative potential.

Naturally, any of these aspects of the animus can be projected onto an outer man. As with the projected anima, this can lead to unrealistic expectations and acrimony in relationships. Jung writes:

> Like the anima, the animus is a jealous lover. He is adept at putting, in place of the real man, an opinion about him, the exceedingly disputable grounds for which are never submitted to criticism. Animus opinions are invariably collective, and they override individuals and individual judg-

---

[31] Ibid., par. 33.

ments in exactly the same way as the anima thrusts her emotional antici-
pations and projections between man and wife.[32]

While a man's task in assimilating the effects of the anima involves
discovering his true feelings, a woman generally becomes familiar with
the nature of the animus by questioning her ideas and opinions.

> The technique of coming to terms with the animus is the same in principle
> as in the case of the anima; only here the woman must learn to criticize
> and hold her opinions at a distance; not in order to repress them, but, by
> investigating their origins, to penetrate more deeply into the background,
> where she will then discover the primordial images, just as the man does
> in his dealings with the anima.[33]

The bottom line in terms of the contrasexual complexes, anima and
animus, is that their projection, from one side or another, is both a common cause of animosity and a singular source of vitality. I think Jung
puts it rather well:

> When animus and anima meet, the animus draws his sword of power and
> the anima ejects her poison of illusion and seduction. The outcome need
> not always be negative, since the two are equally likely to fall in love.[34]

---

[32] "Anima and Animus," *Two Essays on Analytical Psychology*, CW 7, par. 334.
[33] "Anima and Animus," ibid., par. 336.
[34] "The Syzygy: Anima and Animus," *Aion*, CW 9ii, par. 30.

4
Getting a Handle on Eros

Where love reigns, there is no will to power;
And where the will to power is paramount, love is lacking.
—C.G. Jung.

At the end of a long life that included a marriage and many close relationships with women, Jung wrote:

> I falter before the task of finding the language which might adequately express the incalculable paradoxes of love. . . . In my medical experience as well as in my own life I have again and again been faced with the mystery of love, and have never been able to explain what it is. Like Job, I had to "lay my hand on my mouth. I have spoken once, and I will not answer." (Job 40:4f) Here is the greatest and smallest, the remotest and nearest, the highest and lowest, and we cannot discuss one side of it without also discussing the other. No language is adequate to this paradox.[35]

In my own life, quite a few lovelies have come and gone—some come because they liked who they thought I was, then gone because they didn't like who I really was. Or for similar reasons, I left them. In Jung-speak, we call this process withdrawing projections. It can be very painful for all concerned, but it is part and parcel of growing up, and as noted here earlier it is what leads to the end of many relationships.

For my part, and strictly between us, I have lost my heart to more than one lovely because I am temperamentally prone to be caught in that age-old psychological loop: love me please!—a plea doomed to be thwarted when it is not love at all, but need masquerading as lust. Of course I did not know this for the longest time, did not know anything at all as a matter of fact, except that $e = mc^2$, which didn't get me very far with the lovelies in university who were actually more interested in jocks with tidy buns than a nerdy physics major who could barely jitterbug. Never mind, I wasn't ready for them then anyway.

And yet, in later years, that famous Einsteinian equation—that energy

---

[35] *Memories, Dreams, Reflections*, pp. 353f.

is equivalent to mass times the speed of light squared—became so prominent in my thinking that it virtually governed my life, for I associated it with Jung's dictum to go where your energy wants to go.

To my mind, that is the essence of what is involved in what Jung called the process of individuation, and I often shout it from the rooftops: "Follow your energy where it wants to go!" My other mantra, as already noted, is "Do what is right in front of you." As long as you attend to these, I reckon you are on your rightful path.

"And what if you don't know where your energy wants to go," they cry from the cheap seats, "or if it doesn't want to go anywhere?"

Well, don't fret, don't sweat; just hunker down and eat your liver until something happens to wake you up. You can't run a car on blueberry muffins and you can't individuate by will power.

Nurse Pam popped in just then for a visit. She held my hand and stroked my brow, which tends to get fevered when I'm on a rant. Then she kneaded my shoulders, which had more knots than the rope on a schooner.

"You are so beautiful," I said, "and I am just a nothing, a troll. I can hardly believe you really like me."

"More than like, you silly," said Pam, poking me and tucking her head under my chin. "You are actually quite something. You are seductive without even trying. You give me heart, and I've given you a big piece of mine," she said, lowering her eyes. "When I'm with you, the whole concept of time seems different . . . it stops but moves . . . do you know what I mean? I think that loving you has done wonderful things for my ease in life . . . If my situation were different . . . well, you know. . . ."

She didn't need to spell it out. Her "situation" included a family and a home she was very attached to. I accepted that and it had never been an issue between us—I mean it didn't stop us from feeling close and dancing to ol' Blue Eyes in my kitchen. It only stopped us from going to bed together, a loss that neither of us begrudged. Indeed, with Pam's blessing I found another outlet for that kind of libido.

"You could find someone else to bonk," she said, "I'd be okay with that."

I wasn't sure she meant it, but my hormones took me out looking, and before long I chanced upon MP (My Paramour)—a demure, mature Botticelli beauty who happily had a creative connection with her inner man. She too was married, but so what; I knew from our first touch that we would be a good fit, and so we proved to be. For months I romanced her with flowers and letters and long walks arm in arm. Sparks, giggles, the whole ball of wax! And when finally she yielded, her passionate nature bowled me over. She embodied the opposites: shy and bold, modest and shameless. More: she did not stint in expressing her feelings. Before long I was besotted—she was forever on my mind and I lived from tryst to tryst. I wallowed in eros.

MP did not object to my ongoing friendship with Nurse Pam, and Pam applauded my choice. And so we all rejoiced and life was a treat. Well, until MP read *Not the Big Sleep*. "It's very clever," she said, "but why did you give a loverNot a higher status than a lover?"[36]

I gulped. Why indeed? I felt unmasked, a fraud.

"Don't believe everything you read," I said lamely. "That was a theoretical observation, before I met you. You are my sweetheart, the tops. I love you to distraction. You are so precious to me that I can hardly speak," I stammered. "Push come to shove, loverNots can fend for themselves."

Granted, this was short-changing Nurse Pam, but what can you do—lovers *do* come first. Phallos will have its say.[37] You've probably heard the old wives' tale that the way to a man's heart is through his stomach. Well, forget it! I have long observed and experienced that it's rather through his loins. Not that I don't appreciate a tasty meal, but personally, I have fallen somewhat in love with just about every woman I've slept with. You can put that down to my mother complex, or whatever else you fancy; me, I have long since stopped trying to figure it out psychologically; now I just live with that as one of the many "just so" facts of my reality, my fate, myself.

---

[36] See *Not the Big Sleep*, page 81: "A loverNot is at the top of the food chain! She is soul mate, soul friend and sweetheart all in one. A single loverNot, all by herself, is a trinity of anima figures. She gives substance to a man's inner harem."

[37] See Eugene Monick, *Potency: Masculine Aggression as a Path to the Soul,* passim.

MP smiled at me and downcast her eyes, as she was wont to do when nonplussed. I took her in my arms and stroked her hair, and went on speaking to her: "If I were to hold your hand and touch the ends of your fingers, you would feel me touching your toes. A little higher, on two fingers, and you would feel me touching your calves. I would touch your knuckles and you would feel me touching your knees. Higher still, the fleshy part of the top of your fingers, and you would feel me touching your thighs. Then I would pull your hand toward me and kiss between your fingers ..."

MP was trembling. Me too. We went to bed and made love listening to Eva Cassidy torching one of MP's favorites:

> Before the day I met you,
> Life was so unkind.
> Now you're the key to my peace of mind,
> For you make me feel like a natural woman.
>
> When my soul was in the lost and found,
> You came along to claim it.
> I didn't know just what was wrong with me,
> Your kisses helped me name it.
> Now I'm no longer doubtful of what I'm living for,
> And if I make you happy,
> I don't need to do more.
> 'cause you make me feel like a natural woman.[38]

And soon thereafter came the *relationus interruptus* occasioned by my bypass surgery and the wee stroke, and the weeks recovering. I rested a lot, stared at the wall, amd thought about what I wanted to do with the rest of my life. As if I were in charge.

Back home at last, one evening I read to Nurse Pam some of what I'd written about my experiences in the hospital, as recounted here earlier.

"It gives me a twinge," said Pam. "I wish I could have been there more for you. Just imagine how your other lovelies will feel when they read it. It's a journey we couldn't take but those who love you will wince

---

[38] "Natural Woman," on *No Boundaries.* Lyrics by Tony Taylor (Seakara Tunes Publishing, ASCAP).

for not being able to go through it step by step."

Jeez! "That never occurred to me," I said, for it hadn't.

Pam said: "I am not surprised that you wouldn't think of the poor lovelies twinging at your experience of the knife. You carry on like the brave knight battling off the IVs with nary a self-pitying thought . . . but then you see, the twinge is eclipsed by the lovelies' sighs at the bravado and diffidence to the brave knight's suffering. My, but you do have a grip on this fairy-tale thing!"

I grimaced. I didn't know what to say because my mind was crowded with things to write. As a matter of fact, when I was in the hospital I asked MP not to visit, thinking to save her the pain of seeing me in a stricken state. Months later, she told me she had taken that to mean I no longer cared for her, which distressed her a lot more than seeing me would have. Oh, what a chump I am when it comes to reading women.

At last I said to Pam: "Hey, in describing my time in rehab, I was just playing for laughs . . ."

"Well, yes, I did laugh too," she smiled, hugging me, "but it was no joke at the time. You might have died!"

I replied: "It was no joke to me either, but I have some distance from it now and so I can play with the experience. That's what writers do, you know."

Nurse Pam pulled me close. Holy Petunia! Her body fit into mine like hand into glove. I could hardly stand the thrill of it. I was about to take other liberties when she looked at her watch and held me at a distance.

"LoverNot!" she cried. "I have to go now." And she pecked my cheek and fled into the night, jetting off in her little fire-engine-red Neon.

I stayed up for awhile trying to make sense of that experience and what my true feelings were. I think that men generally know right away what they think about something, but they often don't know how they feel, and particularly what goes on between them and their lady friends. They need time to digest what happens in intimate encounters. Lessons learned: woman, don't press your man for how he feels; man, hold your tongue for a while.

Well, skoot, I was in the same precarious boat, not at all holier than thou or them. Like anyone intent on becoming conscious, I was and am obliged to differentiate between love and lust and all the gray areas in between. Sink or swim. You sink—overwhelmed by life as you find it—if you remain unreflective, unconscious. You swim if you start paying attention to what happens to you day by day. And you can't get out of the pool until you've done at least 300 laps, bare-assed . . . oh, pardon me, I got carried away.

Now, it is true that a year or so ago I proposed marriage to Nurse Pam.[39] I guess I should clear that up right away. We had accumulated a pile of good feelings for each other that I thought had to go somewhere, escalate to a new plane, as it were. Pam took my proposal to heart and gave it serious consideration. However, we soon came to our senses and realized that the relationship we had was plenty good enough. Marry? Arrgghhh! Live together? Arrgghhh! She wanted to keep what she had, and I liked being single and living alone. So we settled happily back into being affectionate loverNots and close-dancing in the kitchen to Frankie, dear ol' Blue eyes:

> You and the night and the music
> Fill me with flaming desire,
> Setting my feelings completely on fire.
> You and the night and the music
> Thrill me, but will we be one,
> After the night and the music are done?[40]

Meanwhile, MP declared that she didn't have a jealous bone in her body and suggested that the three of us go to bed with a lobster and a dish of melted butter. The idea was mildly erotic, but I knew that in practice it would simply be too darn messy. Just because I have a soft spot for intuitives doesn't mean that I have to go along with all their nutty ideas, which by and large are spawned by their immersion in the world of limitless possibilities. "Good for them!" I can say, but I'm not like that at all. I am a dyed-in-the-wool sensation type, grounded—nay, cemented—in the mundane. As noted elsewhere and often, I do what is

---

[39] See *Not the Big Sleep*, pp. 112ff.

[40] "You and the Night and the Music," on *Frank Sinatra: Romance*. Lyrics by Arthur Schwartz and Howard Dietz (Warner Bros. Inc./Arthur Schwartz Music Ltd.).

right in front of me, and if I have an idea of what to do next I better act on it right away, for I might forget about it tomorrow and not get another idea for a month. But lobster in bed? Not on your life. And I'm not really interested in threesomes anyway.

Intuitives are the Trojan horses of life, ambushing others with the lure of what's possible. Sensation types can focus and get things done, but otherwise they tend to be sticks in the mud, party poopers. The two types are shadow brothers—or sisters. Which means they are fated to fall in love—or hate each other. And I've been on both ends of that stick. That's why my life is pretty much taken up with the study of the union of opposites—well, when I'm not submerged in eros up to my ears.

Here's Frankie again:

> I have been a rover,
> I have walked alone,
> Hiked a hundred highways,
> Never found a home.
> Still and all I'm happy,
> The reason is, you see, that
> Once in a while,
> Love's been good to me.[41]

Well, perhaps that's the refrain of every Don Juan whose secret, unconscious wish is to stop hiking. And so what? So I'll keep it in mind. And meanwhile, there is no denying that the passionate commingling of man and woman is what keeps the human race alive.

---

[41] "Love's Been Good to Me," ibid. Lyrics by Rod McKuen.

5
A Typological Compass

I was thunderbolted when I realized that the problems between my wife and I were due to some extent because we were typologically different. I had no idea. Well, I was also psychologically naïve in many other ways, so no surprise there. For instance, I did not know of the woman in me or of the man lurking behind my wife's smiling face and often out to get me. These two invisible partners often wreaked havoc on our relationship. More about that later, but first let's look at typology, which is such a prominent factor in the dynamics of relationships.

Why do we move through life the way we do? Why do some of us prefer to be alone rather than with other people—or at a party instead of reading a book? Why don't we all function in the same way?

From earliest times, attempts have been made to categorize individual attitudes and behavior patterns in order to explain the differences between people. Jung's model of typology is to my mind the best of them. It is the basis for modern "tests" such as the Myers-Briggs Type Indicator (MBTI), used by corporations and institutions in order to classify a person's interests, attitudes and behavior patterns, and hence the type of work or education they might be best suited for.

Jung did not develop his model of psychological types for that purpose, nor do I use it in that way. Rather than label people as this or that type, Jung sought simply to explain the differences between the ways we function and interact with our surroundings in order to promote a better understanding of human psychology in general, and one's own way of seeing the world in particular.

After extensive years of research, Jung identified eight typological groups: two personality attitudes—*introversion* and *extraversion*—and four functions—*thinking, sensation, intuition* and *feeling,* each of which may operate in an introverted or extraverted way.

In Jung's model, introversion and extraversion are psychological modes of adaptation. In the former, the movement of energy is toward the inner world. In the latter, interest is directed toward the outer world. In one case the subject (inner reality) and in the other the object (outer reality) is of primary importance. Whether one is predominately introverted or extraverted—as opposed to what one is doing at any particular time—depends on the direction one's energy naturally, and usually, flows.[42]

Each of the four functions has its special area of expertise. *Thinking* refers to the process of cognitive thought; *sensation* is perception by means of the physical sense organs; *feeling* is the function of subjective judgment or valuation; and *intuition* refers to perception via the unconscious.

Briefly, the sensation function establishes that something exists, thinking tells us what it means, feeling tells us what it's worth to us, and through intuition we have a sense of what can be done with it (the possibilities).

No one function by itself (and neither attitude alone) is sufficient for ordering our experience of ourselves or the world around us. Says Jung:

> For complete orientation all four functions should contribute equally: thinking should facilitate cognition and judgment, feeling should tell us how and to what extent a thing is important or unimportant for us, sensation should convey concrete reality to us through seeing, hearing, tasting, etc., and intuition should enable us to divine the hidden possibilities in the background, since these too belong to the complete picture of a given situation.[43]

In everyday usage, the feeling function is often confused with an emotional reaction. Emotion, more properly called affect, is invariably the

---

[42] Note that introversion is quite different from introspection, which refers to self-examination. Although introverts may have more time or inclination for introspection than do extraverts, introverts have no monopoly on psychological awareness.

[43] "Definitions," *Psychological Types,* CW 6, par. 900. Jung acknowledged that the four orienting functions do not contain everything in the conscious psyche. Will power and memory, for instance, are not included in his model, because although they may be affected by the way one functions typologically, they are not in themselves typological determinants.

result of an activated complex, which is accompanied by noticeable physical symptoms. When not contaminated by a complex, feeling—which tells you what something or someone is worth to you—can in fact be quite cold and dispassionate.

Jung's basic model, including the relationship between the four functions, is a quaternity. In the following diagram, thinking is arbitrarily placed at the top; any of the other functions might be put there, according to which one a person most favors.

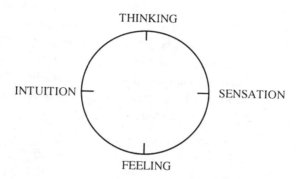

Typologically, opposites can attract or repel. Hence it is common for someone with a dominant thinking function, for instance, to be attracted to a feeling type—or dislike such a person because of his or her very differentness. Similarly, intuitives may be drawn to, or distance themselves from, those with a good sensation function, and vice versa. A better understanding of these opposites—latent or dormant in ourselves—can mitigate such reactions, which often have little or nothing to do with the reality of the other person.

To my mind, Jung's model is most helpful when it is used not as a way to classify oneself or others, but rather in the way he originally thought of it, as a psychological compass. So, in any problematic situation, I ask myself these questions:

1) What are the facts? (sensation)
2) Have I thought it through? (thinking)
3) What is it worth to me to pursue this? (feeling)

4) What are the possibilities? (intuition)

The answers aren't always clear, but the questions keep me on my toes. That is by and large why I don't favor type tests. Type tests concretize what is inherently variable, and thereby overlook the dynamic nature of the psyche. Jung himself said that "the type is nothing static. It changes in the course of life."[44]

Any system of typology is no more than a gross indicator of what people have in common and the differences between them. Jung's model is no exception. It is distinguished solely by its parameters—the two attitudes and the four functions. What it does not and cannot show is the uniqueness of the individual. Also, no one is a pure type. It would be foolish to even try to reduce an individual personality to this or that, just one thing or another. Each of us is a conglomeration, an admixture of attitudes and functions that in their combination defy classification. All that is true, and emphatically acknowledged by Jung—

> One can never give a description of a type, no matter how complete, that would apply to more than one individual, despite the fact that in some ways it aptly characterizes thousands of others. Conformity is one side of a man, uniqueness is the other.[45]

—but it does not obviate the practical value of his model, particularly when one has run aground on the shoals of one's personal psychology.

Whether Jung's model is "true" or not—objectively true—is a moot point. (Indeed, is anything ever "objectively" true?) The real truth is that Jung's model of psychological types has all the advantages and disadvantages of any scientific model. Although lacking statistical verification, it is equally hard to disprove. But it accords with experiential reality. Moreover, since it is based on a fourfold—mandala-like—way of looking at things that is archetypal, it is psychologically satisfying.

As mentioned earlier, one's behavior can be quite misleading in determining typology. For instance, to enjoy being with other people is

44 "The 'Face to Face' Interview," in William McGuire and R.F.C. Hull, eds., *C.G. Jung Speaking*, p.435.
45 "Definitions," *Psychological Types,* CW 6, par. 895.

characteristic of the extraverted attitude, but this does not automatically mean that a person who enjoys lots of company is an extraverted type. Naturally, one's activities will to some extent be determined by typology, but the interpretation of those activities in terms of typology depends on the value system behind the action. Where the subject—oneself—and a personal value system are the dominant motivating factors, there is by definition an introverted type, whether at a party or alone. Similarly, when one is predominantly oriented to the object—things and other people—there is an extraverted type, whether in a crowd or on one's own. This is what makes Jung's system primarily a model of *personality* rather than of behavior.

Everything psychic is relative. I cannot say, think or do anything that is not colored by my particular way of seeing the world, which in turn is a manifestation of both my typology and my complexes. This psychological rule is analogous to Einstein's famous theory of relativity in physics, mentioned earlier—$E=mc^2$—and equally as significant.

Being aware of the way I tend to function makes it possible for me to assess my attitudes and behavior in a given situation. It enables me both to compensate for my personal disposition and to appreciate someone who does not function as I do—someone who may have, per chance, a strength or facility I myself lack.

Typologically speaking,, the important question is not whether one is innately introverted or extraverted, or which function is superior or inferior, but, more pragmatically: in *this* situation, with *that* person, how did I function and with what effect? Did my actions truly reflect my judgments (thinking and feeling) and perceptions (sensation and intuition)? And if not, why not? What complexes were activated in me? To what end? How and why did I mess things up? What does this say about my psychology? What can I do about it? What do I *want* to do about it?

These are among the questions we must take to heart if we want to be psychologically conscious.

The fly in the typology ointment is the shadow, which turns just about everything inside out. I will address that in a later chapter.

6
The Archetypally Complex Journey

Wrestling with your typological orientation is a good start in understanding who you are. But it is child's play compared to becoming acquainted with your complexes.

Complexes are normal and present in everyone; they are the building blocks of the personality. Just as atoms and molecules are the invisible components of physical objects, so complexes are the hidden parts of ourselves; they comprise our identity and are what makes us tick.

When I first went into analysis I knew nothing about complexes. I had heard the word, usually in a pejorative context, but I did not know what it meant. I had read about the Oedipus complex, which seemed to have something to do with a man's unconscious desire to kill his father so he could have his mother all to himself. Well, that was Freud.

Immersing myself in Jung, I learned that complexes are essentially feeling-toned ideas that over the years accumulate around certain images, for instance those of "mother," "father," "money," "power" and so on. I also learned that they have a so-called archetypal core: that is, behind emotional associations with the personal mother, say, there is the archetype of the mother—an age-old collective image spanning the opposites, from nourishment and security ("positive" mother) to devouring possessiveness ("negative" mother).

The notion of archetypes was puzzling until I absorbed the following:

[Archetypes] are, indeed, an instinctive *trend,* as marked as the impulse of birds to build nests, or ants to form organized colonies.[46]

Archetypes are systems of readiness for action, and at the same time images and emotions. They are inherited with the brain structure—indeed they are its psychic aspect.[47]

---

[46] Jung, "Approaching the Unconscious," *Man and His Symbols,* p. 69.
[47] "Mind and Earth," *Civiliaztion in Transition,* CW 10, par. 53.

It is not . . . a question of inherited *ideas* but of inherited *possibilities* of ideas. Nor are they individual acquisitions but, in the main, common to all, as can be seen from [their] universal occurrence.[48]

Archetypes . . . present themselves *as ideas and images,* like everything else that becomes a content of consciousness.[49]

Jung used the simile of the spectrum to illustrate the difference between instinct and the archetype as an "instinctual image":

The dynamism of instinct is lodged as it were in the infra-red part of the spectrum, whereas the instinctual image lies in the ultra-violet part. . . . The realization and assimilation of instinct never take place at the red end, i.e., by absorption into the instinctual sphere, but only through integration of the image which signifies and at the same time evokes the instinct.[50]

INSTINCTS	**ARCHETYPES**
infrared —————————————	————————— ultraviolet
(**Physiological:** body	(**Psychological:** spirit,
symptoms, instinctual	dreams, conceptions,
perceptions, etc.)	images, fantasies, etc.)

So, to sum up, an archetype is a primordial, structural element of the human psyche, an instinctive, universal tendency to form certain ideas and images and to behave in certain ways. I could follow that. However, I still did not connect complexes with my own life and what they had to do with me finding myself on my knees. Then I did Jung's Word Association Experiment, a "test" he developed to illustrate how unconscious factors can disturb the workings of consciousness.

In the Word Association Experiment there is a list of a hundred words, to each of which you are asked to respond with what first comes into your head. The delay in responding (the response time) is measured with

---

[48] "Concerning the Archetypes and the Anima Concept," *The Archetypes and the Collective Unconscious,* CW 9i, par. 136.

[49] "On the Nature of the Psyche," *The Structure and Dynamics of the Psyche,* CW 8, par. 435.

[50] Ibid., par. 414.

a stopwatch, as for instance:

"Head"—"bed" (0.8 sec.)
"Marry"—"together" (1.7 sec.)
"Woman"—"friend" (2 sec.)
"Home"—(long pause) "none" (5.6 sec.)

—and so on.

Then you go through the list a second time, noting different responses to the same words. Finally you are asked for comments on those words to which you had a longer-than-average response time, a merely mechanical response, or a different association on the second run-through. All these had been flagged by the questioner as "complex indicators."

It was an illuminating experience. It was also deflating. It convinced me that complexes were not only real but were alive in me and quite autonomous, independent of my will. I realized they could affect my memory, my thoughts, my moods, my behavior. I was not free to be me—there *was* no "me"—when I was in the grip of a complex.

Freud described dreams as the *via regia,* the royal road, to the unconscious. Jung showed that the royal road to the unconscious is rather the complex, the architect of both dreams and symptoms. In fact, Jung originally gave the name "complex psychology" to his school of thought, to distinguish it from Freud's school of psychoanalysis.

The activation of a complex is always marked by the presence of some strong emotion, whether it be love, hate, anger, sadness or joy. Everyone is complexed by something, which is to say that we all react emotionally when the right buttons are pushed. Or, to put it another way, an emotional reaction—think of tears welling up, or spontaneous laughter—*means* that a complex has been activated. When we are emotional we can't think straight and hardly know how we feel. We speak and act out of the complex, and when it has run its course we may well wonder what took over.

We cannot get rid of our complexes because they are deeply rooted in our personal history. Complexes are part and parcel of who we are. The most we can do is become aware of how we are influenced by them and how they interfere with our conscious intentions. As long as we are unconscious of our complexes, we are prone to being overwhelmed or driven by them. When we understand them, their power to affect us is diminished. They do not disappear but over time their grip may loosen.

Life would be very dull without complexes. They are the very stuff of history and drama, films, novels and TV sitcoms. On the personal level they can either spice our relationships with love or poison them with resentment, irritation, self-pity, anxiety, fear and guilt.

A complex is a bundle of associations, sometimes painful, sometimes joyful, always accompanied by affect. It has energy and a life of its own. It can upset digestion, breathing and the rate at which the heart beats. It behaves like a partial personality. When you want to say or do something and a complex interferes, you find yourself saying or doing something quite different from what you intended. Your best intentions are upset, just as if you had been interfered with by another person.

In some conditions, schizophrenia for example, complexes emancipate themselves from conscious control to such an extent that they can become visible and audible. They appear as visions and speak in voices that are like those of definite people. But this is not in itself pathological. Complexes are regularly personified in dreams, and one can train oneself so they become visible or audible also in a waking condition. It is even psychologically healthy to do so, for when you give them a voice, a face, a personality, they are less likely to take over when you're not looking.

We like to think we are masters in our own house, but clearly we are not. We are renters at best. Psychologically we live in a boarding house of saints and knaves, nobles and villains, run by a landlord who for all we know is indifferent to the lot. We fancy we can do what we want, but when it comes to a showdown our will is hampered by fellow boarders with a mind of their own.

To sum up: complexes have a tendency to live their own lives in spite of our conscious intentions. Our personal unconscious consists of an unknown number of these fragmentary personalities. This actually explains a lot that is otherwise quite puzzling, like the fact that one is able to dramatize mental contents. When someone creates a character on the stage, or in a poem or novel, it is not simply a product of that person's imagination. Writers may deny that their work has a psychological meaning, but in fact you can read their mind when you study the characters they create.

Marie-Louise von Franz, the doyenne of Jungian analysts until her death in 1998, once told me of a man who after two years of bringing his dreams for analysis confessed that he had made them all up. "The joke's on you," she said to him. "Where do you think they came from? You said what was in you. That's as real as any dream."

Enough talk. I wanted to wallow in emotion. So sue me. I put on Eva Cassidy and thought of my winsome paramour.

> My heart goes crazy, crazy for you.
> I can't explain, it's just the way that you are.
> Walking hand in hand, not a care in the world.
> In the middle of a storm,
> I can't seem to find my way
> Till I see you reaching out to me.....
> You are the one,
> My heart goes crazy,
> I can't explain,
> It's just the way that you are.[51]

Okay, we know all about projection. So maybe my feelings for MP won't last, or in time she'll become indifferent to me. But that doesn't matter! What matters is honoring how you feel when you feel it, instead of cutting it off at the knees.

---

[51] "You Are," on *No Boundaries.* Lyrics by Tony Taylor, published Seakara Times Publishing (ASCAP).

7
Shadow Boxing

Jung's model of typology is a valuable guide to our dominant psychological disposition, the way we mostly are. It also reveals, by inference, the way we mostly aren't—but could also be.

Where, then, is the rest of us (mostly)?

Theoretically, we can say that the inferior or undeveloped attitude and functions are part of that side of ourselves Jung dubbed the shadow. The reason for this is both conceptual and pragmatic.

Conceptually, the shadow, like the ego, is a complex, an agglomeration of associations. But where the ego, as the dominant complex of consciousness, is associated with aspects of oneself that are more or less known (as "I"), the shadow consists of personality characteristics that are not part of one's usual way of being in the world, and therefore are more or less alien to one's sense of personal identity.

The shadow is potentially both creative and destructive: creative in that it represents aspects of oneself that have been buried or that might yet be realized; destructive in the sense that its value system and motivations tend to undermine or disturb one's conscious image of oneself.

Everything that is not ego is relatively unconscious; hence before the contents of the unconscious have been differentiated, the shadow *is*, in effect, the unconscious. In terms of typology, since the opposite attitude and the inferior functions are by definition relatively unconscious, they are naturally tied up with the shadow.

In one's immediate world, there are attitudes and behavior that are socially acceptable, and those that are not. In our formative years it is natural to suppress the unacceptable aspects of ourselves. They "fall into" the unconscious and become aspects of our shadow. What is left is the persona—the "I" one presents to the outside world.

The persona would live up to what is expected, what is proper. It is both a useful bridge socially and an indispensable protective covering;

without a persona, we are simply too vulnerable. We regularly cover up our weaknesses with a persona, since we do not like them to be exposed.

Civilized society depends on interactions between people through the persona. But it is psychologically unhealthy to identify with it, to believe that we are exactly or only the person we show to others.

Generally speaking, the shadow is less civilized, more primitive and cares little for social propriety. What is of value to the persona is anathema to the shadow and vice versa. Hence the shadow and the persona function in a compensatory way: the brighter the light, the darker the shadow. The more one identifies with the persona—which in effect is to deny that one has a shadow—the more trouble one will have with the unacknowledged areas of the personality. Thus the shadow constantly challenges the morality of the persona, and, to the extent that ego-consciousness identifies with the persona, the shadow also threatens the ego. In the process of psychological development that we call individuation, disidentification from the persona and the conscious assimilation of the shadow go hand in hand. The ideal is to have an ego strong enough to acknowledge both the persona and the shadow without identifying with either.

This is not as easy as it sounds. We tend to identify with what we are good at, and why shouldn't we? The superior function, after all, has an undeniable utilitarian value. It greases the wheels of life and generally brings praise, material rewards and a good deal of satisfaction. Thus it inevitably becomes a prominent aspect of the persona. Why give it up? The answer is that we don't or won't—unless we have to. And when do we "have to"?—when we encounter situations in life that are not amenable to the way we usually function.

In practice, as noted earlier, the shadow and everything associated with it is virtually synonymous with unlived life. "There must be more to life than this," is a remark heard often enough in the analyst's consulting room. All that I consciously am and aspire to be effectively shuts out what I might be, could be, *also am.* Some of what I also am has been repressed because it was or is unacceptable to oneself or others, and some is simply unrealized potential.

Through introspection, we can become aware of shadow aspects of our personality, but we may still resist them or fear their influence. And even where they are known and would be welcome, they are not readily available to the conscious will. For instance, my intuition may be shadowy—primitive and unadapted—so I cannot call it up when it's needed. I may know that feeling is required in a particular situation but for the life of me can't muster it. I want to enjoy the party but my carefree extraverted side has vanished. I may know I'm due for some introversion, but the lure of the bright lights is just too strong.

The shadow does not necessarily demand equal time with the ego, but for a balanced personality it does require recognition. For the introvert this may involve an occasional night on the town—against his better judgment. For the extravert it might involve—in spite of herself—an evening staring at the wall.

In general, the person whose shadow is dormant gives the impression of being dull and stodgy. This is true no matter which attitude is dominant: the extravert seems to lack depth; the introvert appears socially inept, lifeless.

The introvert's psychological situation is laid bare in the writer Franz Kafka's observation:

> Whoever leads a solitary life, and yet now and then wants to attach himself somewhere; whoever, according to changes in the time of day, the weather, the state of his business and the like, suddenly wishes to see any arm at all to which he might cling—he will not be able to manage for long without a window looking on to the street.[52]

Similarly, the extravert may only become conscious of his or her shadow when struck by the vacuity of social intercourse.

There is a balance between introversion and extraversion, as there is between the normally opposing functions, but it rarely becomes necessary—or even possible—to seek it out, until and unless the conscious ego-personality falls on its face. In that case, which happily manifests as a nervous breakdown rather than a more serious psychotic break, the

---

[52] "The Street Window," in *The Penal Colony:Stories and Short Pieces.* p. 39.

shadow side demands to be recognized. The resulting turmoil is not entirely negative, for it has the advantage of overcoming the tyranny of the dominant attitude of consciousness. If the symptoms are then attended to with some seriousness, the whole personality can be enlivened, or, to put it in theological language, redeemed.

There is by definition a natural conflict between ego and shadow, but when one has made a commitment to live out as much of one's potential as possible, then the integration of the shadow—including one's inferior attitude and functions—evolves from being merely theoretically desirable to becoming a practical necessity. Hence the process of assimilating the shadow may require the capacity to take risks, live somewhat adventurously and with a degree of psychological tension (about which more later).

The introverted man, for instance, under the influence of his inferior extraverted shadow, is prone to imagine he is missing something: vivacious women, fast company, excitement. He himself (his ego) may see these as chimeras, but his shadow yearns for them. His shadow may lead him into the darkest venues, and then, as often as not, whimsically abandon him. What is left? A lonely introvert who longs for home.

On top of that, the extraverting introvert who is taken at face value—as a true extravert—is liable to end up in hot water. Whereas the introverting extravert has only himself to deal with, the extraverting introvert often makes a tremendous impact on those who cross his path, but he might not want to be with them the next day. When his introversion reasserts itself, he may literally want nothing to do with other people. Thus the introverted thinking type whose shadow may be a carefree Don Juan, say, wreaks havoc on the vulnerable hearts of others.

True extraverts genuinely enjoy being part of the crowd. That is their natural home. They are restless alone, not because they are avoiding themselves, but because they have few parameters for establishing their identity outside of a group. The introverted shadow of extraverts may encourage them to stay home and find out who they are. But just as introverts may be abandoned by their shadows in a noisy bar, so extraverts may be left high and dry—feeling very lonely—when on their own.

The opposite attitude and the inferior functions are commonly personified as shadow figures in dreams and fantasies. Dream activity becomes heightened when a function not usually available to consciousness is required. Thus a man who is a thinking type, after a quarrel with his mate, for instance, may be assailed in his dreams by images of primitive feeling persons, dramatically illustrating a side of himself still unassimilated. Similarly, the sensation type stuck in a rut may be confronted in dreams by an intuitive friend showing new possibilities.

To assimilate or develop a function means to live with it in the foreground of consciousness. A minor sop is not enough. For instance, von Franz writes that "if [an intuitive] does a little cooking or sewing, it does not mean that the sensation function has been assimilated." She goes on:

> Assimilation means that the whole adaptation of conscious life, for a while, lies on that one function. Switching over to an auxiliary function takes place when one feels that the present way of living has become lifeless, when one gets more or less constantly bored with oneself and one's activities. . . . The best way to know how to switch is simply to say, "All right, all this does not mean anything to me any more. Where in my past life is an activity that I feel I could still enjoy? An activity out of which I could still get a kick?" If a person then genuinely picks up that activity, he will see that he has switched over to another function.[53]

---

[53] *Jung's Typology,* p. 59.

8
Heroism Unmasked

The more I work with people analytically, the more simple-minded I become: I throw theory out the window; no couch, no technique, just him or her and me, sitting across from each other, face to face. Often we don't know what to say, or just can't find the right words for what's going on in us. They are generally looking to cure what ails them. I know there is no quick fix and so I am seeking a relationship, which may, if we're lucky (*Deo concedente,* we say: God willing*)*, result in alleviating their miseries. It's always touch and go. I touch and they go, or vice versa. Mine is an interesting profession, which I pursue alternately with confidence and doubt. I hold the tension between these opposites, among others, as best I can.

I think it is not generally realized that those who go into analysis, or otherwise determine to get to know themselves, are embarking on a hero's journey. To understand what this means involves thinking symbolically or metaphorically rather than literally.

For instance, being crippled is an apt metaphor for those who find themselves in a psychological crisis. Broken in spirit, unable to function in their usual way, they are "on their knees"; they want to pull themselves together, get back on their feet. Meanwhile, they "limp along." I have been there; that's how I came to do what I do. Being an analyst is a vocation, and not entirely altruistic. Working with others is a way of working on myself.

In mythology, the motif of the cripple is everywhere. There is the lame Hephaestus, blacksmith to the gods; the Grail legend's fisher king with a gimpy leg; a string of wounded Mesopotamian kings; Pan with goats' feet; Osiris who lost his penis; Harpocrates, son of Isis and Osiris; Mani, the founder of Manichaeism; the Egyptian god Bes, and so on. Being crippled, blind or otherwise incapacitated is often a sign of chthonic (earthy) wisdom, as in legends of dwarfs and dactyls, and the

Cabiri, sons of Hephaestus. On the whole, crippledom seems to be an archetypal image of one's fate, for it is historically and traditionally associated with heroes.

It is a hero's task to do something out of the ordinary. For those in analysis this means trying to understand why they act or react the way they do. This may alienate them from their peers and colleagues, but one gets used to that if you'd rather muse over a dream than watch a basketball match, play bridge or embroider a quilt. Dreams, and often outer life too, take on the flavor of a myth or a fairy tale. There are wicked witches (negative mothers) and fairy godmothers (positive mothers); wizards and elves, demons and wise old men (aspects of the father); helpful animals (instincts) to guide one through the forest of daily life. There are rolling balls and skeins of thread (markers on the way); magic hats and cloaks (appropriate attitudes); thorns and needles that prick (projections); giants (complexes) that knock you off your feet (your standpoint); princesses (feminine energy) held captive in towers and princes (masculine energy) scaling mountains to rescue them.

That's just for starters. As a matter of fact, I have never come across a motif in a dream that could not also be found in a myth, legend or fairy tale. This is one of the best-kept secrets of psychological development: our forebears in faraway times went through the same tortuous trials as do we. And some of them survived to tell about it.

A sword-fight in a dream may reflect the cut-and-thrust of an encounter with your boss; the thorn hedge that protects a sleeping beauty is the prickly animus who keeps a woman's beaus at bay; the ravishing vixen who lures you to bed may be a false bride (about which more in the next chapter); the secretary guarding the photocopier is a siren in high heels; an outworn conscious attitude is a sickly old king; an absent queen reflects lack of feeling; a quarrelsome royal couple is a conflict between masculine and feminine, ego and anima/animus; nightmares of burglars breaking in suggest shadow sides of oneself demanding recognition; and on and on.

Like the Dummling or youngest brother in many fairy tales, it is appropriate to be naive about the unconscious and what it holds. This actually works in one's favor, since accomplishing some of the tasks required of us are only possible if we suspend a rational way of looking at things. The Dummling represents an aspect of the individual psyche that has not been coerced by collective pressures. We all had it at first, as children, and still do, though buried under the accretions of daily life: a virgin innocence unhobbled by hard knocks; fresh, spontaneous, and not yet fixed in rigid patterns; a time when the border between fantasy and reality was permeable. That openness to the unknown is an important element in the struggle to discover our own individual truth.

In fairy tales the goal is to find the treasure, the ring, the golden egg, the elixir of life. Psychologically these all come to the same thing: oneself—one's true feelings and unique potential. This pursuit, by whatever name, is a time-honored tradition. It differs greatly in detail, but the pattern is well known; only names, times and places change.

Symbolically, the hero's journey is a round, as illustrated below.[54]

CALL TO ADVENTURE

---

[54] Adapted from Joseph Campbell, *The Hero with a Thousand Faces*, p. 245.

Among other things, the hero's journey involves a dangerous trial of some kind, psychologically analogous, writes Jung, to "the attempt to free ego-consciousness from the deadly grip of the unconscious."[55] It is a motif represented by imprisonment, crucifixion, dismemberment, abduction—the kind of experience weathered by sun-gods and other heroes since time immemorial: Gilgamesh, Osiris, Christ, Dante, Odysseus, Aeneas, as well as Pinocchio and Dorothy in *The Wizard of Oz*. In the language of the mystics it is called the dark night of the soul. In everyday life, we mere mortals know it as a feeling of despair and a desire to call in sick and hide under the covers.

*

I sat back and looked at the computer. All that head stuff tired me out. I longed for a cigarette but I didn't dare. My arteries wouldn't thank me, and anyway my sweetheart MP was allergic to smoke. I poured a stiff Scotch and put on a Sinatra CD that wrenched me into quite another dimension; call it eros or feeling, comes to the same thing. I had MP on my mind, front and center. Frankie put my feelings into words and music:

Never thought I'd fall
But now I hear love's call.
I'm getting sentimental over you.
Things you say and do just thrill me through and through
I'm getting sentimental over you.
I thought I could live without love.
Now I must admit that love is all that I'm thinking of.[56]

Typically, in myth and legend, the hero journeys by ship or braves dark forests, burning deserts, ice fields, etc. He fights a sea monster or dragon, is swallowed, struggles against being bitten or crushed to death, and having arrived inside the belly of the whale, like Jonah, seeks the vital organ and cuts it off, thereby winning release. Eventually the hero must return and bear witness.

---

[55] *Symbols of Transformation*, CW 5, par. 539.
[56] "I'm Getting Sentimental Over You," Lyrics by George Bassman and Ned Washington (ASCAP).

The night sea journey myths, an important subset of these hero tales, derive from the perceived behavior of the sun, which, in Jung's lyrical image, "sails over the sea like an immortal god who every evening is immersed in the maternal waters and is born anew in the morning."[57] The sun going down, analogous to the loss of energy in a depression, is thus the necessary prelude to rebirth. Cleansed in the healing waters, the ego lives again. Or, in another mythological image, it rises from the ashes, like the phoenix.

Psychologically, the whale-dragon-monster is the unconscious, and in particular the parental complexes.[58] The battles and suffering that take place during the night sea journey symbolize the heroic attempt to assimilate unconscious contents instead of being overwhelmed by them. Symbolically, the vital organ that must be severed is the umbilical cord, the regressive tie to the past. The potential result is the release of energy—symbolically, the sun on a new day—that has hitherto been tied up with the complexes.

The hero is the one who conquers the dragon, not the one devoured by it, nor the one who turns tail and goes home to mama. As Jung writes:

> He is no hero who never met the dragon, or who, if he once saw it, declared afterwards that he saw nothing. Equally, only one who has risked the fight with the dragon and is not overcome by it wins the hoard, the "treasure hard to attain." He alone has a genuine claim to self-confidence, for he has faced the dark ground of his self and thereby has gained . . . . an inner certainty which makes him capable of self-reliance.[59]

Few choose the hero's journey. Who would willingly leave the comfort of home for a whale's belly? But when something in us demands the journey, we are obliged to live it out whether we like it or not.

Analysts cannot save people from the hazards to be faced, nor should

---

[57] Ibid., par. 306.

[58] See M. Esther Harding, *The Parental Image: Its Injury and Reconstruction,* for an explication of the *Enuma Elish,* Babylonian legend of the beginnings of consciousness, as a paradigm for the struggle to first overcome and then redeem the parental complexes, pp. 32ff.

[59] *Mysterium Coniunctionis,* CW 14, par. 756.

they even try. What nature has ordained, let no one interfere with. The hero's journey is an inner imperative that must be allowed to run its course. The hero must suffer in order to be redeemed. Perhaps the most analysts can do is to accompany their clients on their unique journey and alert them to some dangers along the way.

Personally, I see what I do as akin to midwifery—assisting at the birth of something new and precious.

9
The Lazarus Heart

I want to say more about Norman, my hapless analysand whose plight I wrote about earlier. After we had been working together for a couple of years, he got it into his head that he wanted to be an analyst. So he applied to the Jung Institute in Zurich, and here's what happened next.

Norman arrived exuberant.

"It's all happening!"

He was barely able to contain himself. He thumped the table between us.

"I'm accepted!" he cried. "Zurich said yes!"

He handed me the letter. The C.G. Jung Institute would be pleased to receive him as a training candidate, beginning the next spring session. That was four months away. Time enough to arrange his life, settle his affairs.

Norman was beside himself with glee. He bowed to me. "I'm sure your letter helped."

He insisted I put some music on. I chose a Mozart flute concerto by the Swiss flautist Peter-Lukas Graf.

"That's nice," said Norman, "but it's the wrong mood. Sting! Play Sting!"

My sons had given me Sting's *Nothing Like the Sun* for Christmas. I put it on and we listened to the first track, "The Lazarus Heart":

> He looked beneath his shirt today
> There was a wound in his flesh so deep and wide
> From the wound a lovely flower grew
> From somewhere deep inside
> He turned around to face his mother
> To show her the wound in his breast that burned like a brand
> But the sword that cut him open
> Was the sword in his mother's hand.

Every day another miracle
Not even death could tear us apart
To sacrifice a life for yours
I'd be the blood of the Lazarus heart
The blood of the Lazarus heart.[60]

Norman was quiet now.

"It's the right mood but the words give me the shivers," he said.

I turned it off and looked at him.

"You're a lucky man," I said. "You know your wounds."

"It feels like a mixed blessing," said Norman.

"Give it time; Lazarus was resurrected."

Norman became earnest.

"Speaking of wounds, do you know Somerset Maugham's *Of Human Bondage?*" he asked.

"No," I lied, "tell me."

"I haven't read the book," said Norman, "but last night I saw the film. It's a classic, made in 1934 with Leslie Howard and Bette Davis. It's about a young doctor who falls in love with a street girl. She gets sick and he nurses her back to health. Then she toys with him—flirts with other men, keeps him at a distance and so on. He accepts it all, one shit sandwich after another. He's so besotted he can't see what she is. It's all very sad and romantic—I guess you'd call it a devilish anima fascination. The doctor has a club foot, a wound that will never heal. It reminded me of the fisher king in the Grail legend."

He looked out the window. "And of myself."

I nodded.

"I saw it with Nicole," said Norman. "Remember her? The one with the cape? I walked her home in a drizzle. She huddled close under my umbrella and said how much she enjoyed being with me."

Ah, yes, Nicole. The butterfly waltz and the mulingi shuffle.

"I think I've told you about her penthouse near the university. One big

---

[60] Sting writes: "Lazarus Heart" was a vivid nightmare that I wrote down and then fashioned into a song. A learned friend of mine informs me that it is the archetypal dream of the fisher king. . . . Can't I do anything original?—Sleeve Notes on *Nothing Like the Sun.*

room, not much furniture, abstract paintings on the walls, low lighting. Everything's at floor level, Japanese style. She made us a pot of herb tea. I poked about in her records and put on Crosby, Stills and Nash. I lay on the waterbed listening to "Lady of the Island" and watched Nicole bustle around. I was very happy.

"We drank our tea and smoked a joint, my own home-grown. We giggled a lot. God! Everything's hilarious when you're stoned. We bounced on the bed and pretended we were pirates.

"Nicole put on a flowered kimono and did some T'ai Chi. She's small and thin, very graceful. You'd never know she was over forty. She floated around the room like a hummingbird.

"Then she came to me. She peeled off my clothes and aroused me. That wasn't difficult, but she made it into a ceremony. When I was stiff as a board she got a couple of candles, about the same size as my dick, and set them up on saucers beside the bed. She lit the candles, turned the lights out and stripped off her gown. I was bemused but in no mood to object.

"She sat cross-legged on top of me and wove her fingers through my hair. 'Wicked,' she whispered, 'very wicked!' "

"Wicked?" I repeated.

"I think so," said Norman.

"Maybe it was Wicca," I suggested. "Wicca or *wekken* was a name for the ancient goddess religion, an esoteric cult active in northern Europe for hundreds of years. Some of the women burned as witches in the Middle Ages claimed to belong to it. Maybe it's been revived again. I know a bookstore in California by the name of Feminist Wicca."

Norman shrugged. "Nicole is certainly no feminist. At least not the way I understand it. She's soft and pliant."

Pliant, eh? The word *wych* in Anglo-Saxon meant pliant. Nicole began to interest me.

"She chanted to herself while she fondled me," said Norman.

Casting a spell?

"She'd bring me right to the edge and then stop. Then she'd start again. The candles flickered, casting shadows. The music was low.

"Suite: Judy Blue Eyes" and "Marrakesh Express" went right through me. I was in seventh heaven."

One of the classical attributes of witches was the magic wand, staff or rod. They were said to use it in conjuring up the devil. That's the origin of the modern divining rod for finding water. I wondered: Was Nicole using Norman's member as a stand-in? Maybe that's what today's witches do, what with plastic broom-sticks and all.

According to Funk & Wagnall's *Standard Dictionary of Folklore, Mythology and Legend,* you can spot a witch by some well-known tests.[61] For instance, a witch can't weep; at most she sheds only three tears; she has a birthmark under her armpit or hidden elsewhere under her hair; she has long eyes; she has to stop when she sees a broom and count the straws—or count seeds, grains, holes in a sieve, letters on a written page, etc.

"Long eyes?" said Rachel, rolling hers.

Hey, witches are no joke. They can fly and make themselves invisible. They assume different shapes at will. They have powers of divination and arcane knowledge of drugs. They can inhibit childbirth, cause illness or death and turn men into raving beasts.

Norman was smiling at the ceiling, still on the waterbed. No froth on his lips.

Comforting, but inconclusive.

"Tell me," I said, "Does Nicole have any birthmarks?"

"Not that I've noticed," said Norman. "She has two tattoos, though—a butterfly on one hip . . ."

Butterfly, an ancient image for *psyche,* the Greek word for soul.

". . . and a five-pointed star on the other."

A pentagram! During the middle Ages such figures were scrawled on the doors of those suspected of witchcraft. The witch brigade saw the sign and torched the house.

"Nicole finally took her mount," said Norman. "She squared her shoulders and rode me. In the dim light she even looked like a jockey. She whipped me with a shoelace—honest!—and I responded. Plunging,

---

[61] Maria Leach, ed., *Standard Dictionary of Folklore, Mythology and Legend,* p. 1179.

dipping, a mighty rod of steel. Twisting, turning, a fine fettle of flesh.
Careful, steady, holding, pushing, rolling around . . .

" 'Heigh-ho! Heigh-ho!' she cried, slapping my sides, spurring me on.

"I was galloping now, down the home stretch, pounding the turf, clods
whipping by, neck and neck, the winning post looming, we're at the wire
. . .

" 'Now now!' cried Nicole, reveling, bursting through. 'Yes yes yes
oh yes that's it you win you win,' and we were together, a photo-finish."

Norman wiped his brow.

Of course, I thought, there are white witches too who do nothing but
good.

*

Norman survived Nicole, and so did I. One of the things about being
an analyst is that you get to live vicariously. Every day is a soap opera.
You sit back and listen. You hear it all, the gamut of life, from juicy ex-
ploits to embarrassing disasters. You are there, you feel what it's like,
but you don't get too involved because your own life is not on the line.

Indeed, the great challenge for an analyst is to continue to live his or
her own life. That means not being satisfied with crumbs from the tables
of one's clients. It also includes doing just what we encourage them to
do: keeping a journal, giving serious attention to dreams and emotional
reactions, taking chances.

In the analytic hour, an analyst has an artificial presence courtesy of
the transference. The analyst has a god-like aura and seems invulnerable.
The same is true of doctors, priests, teachers and therapists of any kind.
It's a persona that goes with the territory. There's nothing wrong with it.
It's useful as a protective screen and, as pointed out earlier, it may have
something to do with whatever healing takes place.

Outside the hour, however, analysts are just like anyone else. We shop
for food and do the laundry. We worry about our weight; our socks have
holes; we snore. We have money problems, unruly children, conflicts
that give us sleepless nights. We too have gardens that need tending.

All this has nothing to do with the analytic persona. The analyst who
forgets that is in big trouble.

Analysis is a job. It's interesting work, but it's still a job. It's true that people can be called to it—like Samuel in the Bible being called to serve God—but so can auto mechanics, chartered accountants, hairdressers and pimps be called to their work. The notion that being an analyst is more meaningful than being, say, a lawyer or a stockbroker, is merely a subjective opinion or a cultural prejudice.

Norman didn't realize this. Although his reasons for wanting to train were valid, he was nevertheless to some extent seduced by the persona of the analyst, namely the confident, relatvely uncomplicated front I presented to him. The nature of our relationship precluded my giving him more than a glimpse of who I really was and what my life was like. In his eyes I was someone special. I didn't mind. Part of my job was to accept whatever projection he had on me. I knew that at some point, if he continued to work on himself, he would take it back. I knew too that this might not happen until he sat in what we call "the other chair."

In the meantime, the way Norman sees me is a prominent factor in his motivation to become more conscious; it will get him through some difficult nights.

*

In the following weeks Norman saw a lot of Nicole. Witch or waif, to my mind she was good for Norman. He was enlivened. His guilt-free gambols with her paralleled his growing ability to distance himself from his wife. Nicole was not a substitute for Norman's wife, as so often happens with men who find themselves a new woman but the same old frying pan; she was a different breed of cat.

In terms of his anima development, personified by Jung as Eve, Helen, Mary or Sophia, Norman had left Eve and was high-flying with Helen.

Rachel popped up.

"Yes!" she cried. "I remember the line from Christopher Marlowe's *Faust:* 'All is dross that is not Helen.' I love it!"

"So do I," I smiled. "But a little Helen goes a long way. You can't stick there forever."

Or maybe you can; what do I know? I guess anything is possible.

I went back to my notes.

The stages of the anima described by Jung are helpful, but only as a rule of thumb. In fact, men live psychologically in a harem. Any man may observe this for himself by paying attention to his dreams and fantasies. His soul-image appears in many different forms, just as a woman's femininity may have myriad expressions.

In subhuman guise, the anima may manifest as snake, toad, cat or bird, or on a slightly higher level, as nixie, pixie, mermaid. In human form, to mention only a few personifications modeled on the prominent goddesses in Greek mythology, the anima may appear as Hera, consort and queen; Demeter/Persephone, the mother/daughter team; Aphrodite, the lover; Pallas Athene, carrier of culture and protectress of heroes; Artemis, the stand-offish, maidenly huntress; and Hecate, ruler in the netherworld of magic.

The assimilation of a particular anima-image results in its death, so to speak. That is to say, as one personification of the anima is consciously understood, it is supplanted by another. The previous anima-image is left behind, a precondition for the coming-into-existence of the next. Like the mythical phoenix, the new soul-image rises out of the ashes of the old; or, to use a different metaphor, the man's new wine—his spirit—needs new vessels.

Anima development in a man is thus a continuous process of death and rebirth. An overview of this kind is very important in surviving the transition stage between one anima-image and the next. Just as no real woman relishes being discarded for another, so no anima-figure willingly takes second place to her upstart rival.

In this area, as in so much else involved in a person's psychological development, the good is the enemy of the better. To have contact with your inner woman at all is a blessing; to be tied to one that holds you back is fatal.

While the old soul mate clamors for the attention that now, in order for the man to move on, is due to and demanded by the new one, the man himself is up against it. The struggle is not just an inner, metaphorical one; it also involves his lived relationships with real women.

The resultant suffering and inner turmoil, the tension and sleepless nights, are comparable to what occurs in any conflict-and-decision situation. Inner disputes of this kind can only be resolved through what in religious terminology is called grace. In the language of analytical psychology it is seen as an intervention of the Self, the regulating center of the personality—the transcendent function, the unexpected, the *tertium non datur* (third not given).

The anima-image that must be left behind is characterized in fairy tales as the false bride, while the new one is called the true bride. The essential difference between the two is captured in Marie-Louise von Franz's observation: "The truth of yesterday must be set aside for what is now the truth of one's psychic life."

Jung refers to the "faithless Eros" required for a man to leave his mother, to relinquish the first love of his life.[62] The same thing is necessary when an old and familiar soul mate, one's inner guide in former times, has to be sacrificed.

Rachel reappeared, somewhat distraught.

"It sounds like you're getting ready to trash me," she said.

I hugged her. She cuddled up and listened as I wrote.

Von Franz explains what Jung meant psychologically by "a faithless Eros":

> That would mean the capacity to turn away from time to time from a relationship . . . . The puer aeternus, in the negative sense of the word, very often tends to be too impressed, too weak, and too much of a "good boy" in his relationships, without a quick self-defense reaction where required.[63]

To "turn away" from a relationship doesn't necessarily mean to leave it. It may simply involve paying more attention to oneself than to the other person. But even this much is a heroic feat for a man with a positive mother complex. It requires a ruthlessness that is characteristic of his unsentimental shadow. If he is not up to it—which to someone he's involved with may look like a lack of relatedness, no heart—he will suffer

---

[62] *Aion,* CW 9ii, par. 22.

[63] *The Problem of the Puer Aeternus,* p. 52.

the consequence: loss of soul. In spite of himself, the new anima-image has the energy; she will withhold it unless, and until, he gives in.

The seductive lure of the false bride manifests in real life not only as a tie to an unsuitable woman but also as an inappropriate choice in a conflict-and-decision situation. This is due to the regressive tendencies of the unconscious. Each new stage of development, each foothold on an increase in consciousness, must be wrested anew from the dragon-like grip of the past.

The work on oneself involved in doing this Jung calls *contra naturam*, against nature. That's because nature is essentially conservative. There is a lot to be said for the natural, primitive mind and the instincts that go with it, but not much in terms of consciousness. Writes Jung:

> Whenever a process has reached a culmination as regards either its clarity or the wealth of inferences that can be drawn from it, a regression is likely to ensue.[64]

The individual experiences this as listlessness, an unaccountable loss of energy, or, at the other extreme, as an inflated sense of self-worth.

Inflation is involved here because a man who has won a relationship to his anima, at whatever level, already feels himself to be king of the castle. He could leap mountains, kill seven giants at a blow. And he doesn't need any kind of drug to feel that way.

The great danger in assimilating previously unconscious psychic contents is that you become proud and overconfident, dangerously liable to overextend yourself. The inflated ego believes the war has been won, when only a local battle was fought. Jung describes it like this:

> Paradoxically enough, inflation is a regression of consciousness into unconsciousness. This always happens when consciousness takes too many unconscious contents upon itself and loses the faculty of discrimination, the *sine qua non* of all consciousness.[65]

Jung was referring here to the collective hubris in Western societies that led to the First World War, but the same thing can be seen in the in-

---

[64] *Psychology and Alchemy*, CW 12, par. 239.
[65] Ibid., par. 563.

dividual: war with oneself, inner strife between the old, false bride and the new, true one; a breakdown in functioning due to being maladapted to the changed circumstances of one's inner world; in short, another—or perhaps the first—midlife crisis.

If the individual does not wake up at this point, even worse may result. The further you go in the process of self-discovery, the further there is to fall. As Jung puts it:

> If the demand for self-knowledge is willed by fate and is refused, this negative attitude may end in real death. The demand would not have come to this person had he still been able to strike out on some promising by-path. But he is caught in a blind alley from which only self-knowledge can extricate him. If he refuses this then no other way is open to him. Usually he is not conscious of his situation, either, and the more unconscious he is, the more he is at the mercy of unforeseen dangers: he cannot get out of the way of a car quickly enough, in climbing a mountain he misses his foothold somewhere, out skiing he thinks he can just negotiate a tricky slope, and in an illness he suddenly loses the courage to live. *The unconscious has a thousand ways of snuffing out a meaningless existence with surprising swiftness.*[66]

"That's pretty scary," said Rachel.

"It is," I agreed, "but read the newspaper. It happens every day."

The appearance of a new aspect of the anima, then, whether it wells up within or presents itself as a fascination for a real woman, may be seen as a call to a new level of consciousness. That's the true bride. Whether you embrace it/her or not—actually or symbolically—you have to take the attraction seriously.

Not becoming conscious when you have the possibility of doing so was always accounted by Jung to be the worst sin, for if you don't live up to an inner possibility it turns negative.

Rachel was intrigued.

"I can see there's a difference between what you call a false and a true bride," she said, "but how do you tell one from the other?"

"It's not easy," I said. "They don't come labeled. A lot depends on a

---

[66] *Mysterium Coniunctionis*, CW 14, par. 675 (italics added).

man's age, his position in life and how much work he's done on himself—particularly the extent to which he's already differentiated his soul-image from the other complexes teeming in his psyche.

"Theoretically, there are two basic types of false bride. One is an anima figure—or an actual woman—who leads a man into the fantasy realm, away from timely responsibilities in the outside world. The other is an inner voice—or again a real woman—that would tie a man to his persona when his real task is to turn inward, find out what's behind the face he shows others.

"The first type is commonly associated with the idealistic attitudes of a younger man. You see this in the disinclination to compromise, a rigid response to the reality of everyday life."

"Revolutionaries and anarchists," nodded Rachel, "they would change the world."

"Right," I said. "In any society there is a need for change, but only those who pay their dues have a hope of making it happen. The rest are pissing in the wind."

Rachel crinkled her nose. She's not all that fond of my colloquial expressions.

I said, "The second type of false bride is normally involved with the regressive tendency of the unconscious in later life, when, for the health of the psyche, material values should take second place. Regression is also evident in those who make feverish efforts to reclaim their youth—much younger companions, a compulsion about fitness, hair transplants and so on.

"There's no hard and fast rule, however. An older man with too much unlived life may have to descend into the whore's cellar, so to speak, as part of his individuation process. The younger man with no ideals may be forced to develop some. One must beware, too, of rationalizations that are simply ego wish-fulfillments."

Rachel took that in and asked: "How does all that affect a man's relationships with women?"

"It's no different from any other psychological content," I said. "The bride of either type, when not recognized as an inner reality, appears in the outside world through projection. If a man's anima is lonely and desperate for attention, he is apt to fall in love with dependent women who demand all his time and energy. The man with a mother-bound anima will get tied up with women who want to take care of him. The man not living up to his potential will fall for women who goad him on.

"The bottom line is that whatever qualities a man doesn't recognize in himself—call them shadow, anima, whatever—will confront him in real life. Outer reflects inner, that's the general rule. If there are any psychological rules that are valid always and everywhere, that's one of them."

Rachel frowned. "The way you put it, women are left with a dog's breakfast."

"That's up to them," I said. "They have a choice too. There is no distinction between an unconscious woman and a man's anima. The implication of this psychological reality is that an unconscious woman can be coerced into being whatever a man wants. But it's just as true the other way around. Unconscious men are easily seduced by a woman's animus. In relationships there are no innocent victims."

Rachel registered shock.

"Read all about it," I said, "in Esther Harding's *The Way of All Women*. She put it better than I can. The more differentiated a woman is in her own femininity, her own identity, the more able she is to reject whatever unsuitable role is projected onto her by a man. This forces the man back on himself. If he has the capacity for self-examination and insight, he may discover how he came to have false expectations. Failing inner resources on either side, there is only rancor and animosity."

I reflected.

"A lot of situations like that," I said, "end in separation or divorce. That's disruptive but psychologically not so bad. Many unions limp along in morbid soil to the advantage of no one, least of all the children involved. It is only a tragedy when the opportunity for self-realization is unrecognized or refused, and then repeated."

Now Rachel's head was swimming. I could see it in her eyes. Normally languid pools, they had become fathomless.

"Let's go back to the false and true brides," she said. "Is what one wants a reliable guide?"

"No," I said, "I'm afraid not. Wants are all ego. Over and against what you want is what the unconscious thrusts upon you for the overall good of the psyche. That's the true bride. It usually appears as something new and unexpected. It's an aspect of the Self, the archetype of wholeness.

"This becomes clearer as you pay attention to yourself. Remember the Grail legend, where the fisher king's wound can only be healed if the hero asks the right question? When Parsifal is first confronted with the phenomenon of the Holy Grail, he is overcome with awe and reverence. He doesn't ask what it has to do with him. The Grail vanishes and he has to wander many years through the forest—the unconscious—before he comes upon it again, asks the right question and heals the fisher king.

"Understanding your own psychology, like recognizing the true bride, is a matter of asking the right questions, again and again. Do that long enough and the Self is activated. Von Franz says that having a relationship with the Self is like being in touch with an 'instinct of truth.' There is an immediate awareness of what is right and true for the personality, a truth without reflection:

> One reacts rightly without knowing why, it flows through one and one does the right thing. One says Yes, or No, sometimes doing one thing and sometimes the other, and can carry on without intermission . . . . That is the action of the Self becoming immediate, and only the Self can accomplish this. On a higher level, it is the same thing as being natural and instinctive, when one can discern between the false and the true. . . . With the help of the instinct of truth, life goes on as a meaningful flow, as a manifestation of the Self.[67]

"In practical terms, it comes down to a man knowing what is right for him. 'He has a strong feeling of what should be and what could be,' writes Jung. 'To depart from this divination means error, aberration, illness.'[68]

"That's why Norman may be off to Zurich and not staying with his

---

[67] *Alchemy: An Introduction to the Symbolism and the Psychology,* pp. 172f.

[68] *Psychology and Alchemy,* CW 12, par. 327.

family," I pointed out. "Events in his outer life reflect what's taken place inside. It's not exactly what he wants, but he knows what he needs."

"It seems so ruthless," said Rachel.

"Yes, and it certainly is. But Norman is following his inner truth, his true bride. Like when I left Canada to be a struggling writer. I would not—or could not—have done that without being nudged by my shadow. Norman is in a similar boat. Once you know what you need, you really have no choice."

Rachel was having trouble keeping her eyes open. She'd had enough, and so had I.

"Thus endeth the lesson," I said.

I made a back-up copy and shut the computer down. I stared out the window. Light was breaking in the east. A taxi passed. A garbage truck rumbled through. The paperboy dropped his bundle and moved on.

A glowing sun heaved up, a great semicircle of fire, clearing the decks for a new day. It would be steaming hot, again. I made another note to look into air-conditioning.

I thought of the scarab beetle. As the sacred Khepri, it was worshiped in ancient Egypt as the embodiment of the rising sun and of the supreme creator god Atum. Khepri symbolized the self-regenerating life force, pictured as pushing a ball of excrement in front of it.. In Heliopolis Khepri was seen as the god of transformation and symbol of the birth of the new sun from the womb of Mother Earth.

A vagrant kicked a can. The lady next door padded to the curb in her dressing gown, calling her cat. Two joggers waved at me without breaking stride. I yawned. A passage from Kafka's diary came to mind. I did quote it earlier, but it's one of my favorites and worth repeating:

Whoever leads a solitary life, and yet now and then wants to attach himself somewhere; whoever, according to changes in the time of day, the weather, the state of his business and the like, suddenly wishes to see any arm at all to which he might cling—he will not be able to manage for long without a window looking on to the street.[69]

---

[69] "The Street Window," in *The Penal Colony*, p. 39.

I plugged into Eva Cassidy:

> Let me be your all and all,
> I'll never let you fall.
> I'll be all you'll ever need
> If you trust in me,
> But the only way you'll see
> Is to listen to what your heart is telling you:
> Take that emotional step
> And bring your love to me,
> And my love will be forever yours.
> I wanna be locked in your lovin' arms,
> I'll be right by your side.
> Take that emotional step and fall in love,
> And my love will be
> forever yours.[70]

"Is there a real Nurse Pam?" I've been asked.

"Of course!" I say, "and there's a real Adam Brillig and a real Rachel and a real MP. And a real Norman too. I don't have the imagination to make these people up from scratch. I can embroider on reality, that's all, and try not to drop too many stitches."

Stage left: Rachel clapping. "You are my hero," she says.

Oh, I fell asleep feeling pretty good.

Well, Norman happened to me many years ago. We had much in common, including leaving our young children in search of our own truth. For some years I felt pretty guilty about that, but now I just look at what I have become since, and see how I have been able to contribute to their well-being—emotionally and financially—because when I was on my knees I chose to follow my own path.

I can't say better than that.

---

70 "Emotional Step," on *No Boundaries.* Lyrics by Tony Taylor.

10
Individuation Versus Individualism

What is the difference between individuation and individualism? Or between individuality and individuation? Well, I have a few ideas, but before I have my say, here are some relevant comments by Jung:

> Individualism means deliberately stressing and giving prominence to some supposed peculiarity rather than to collective considerations and obligations. But individuation means precisely the better and more complete fulfilment of the collective qualities of the human being, since adequate consideration of the peculiarity of the individual is more conducive to a better social performance than when the peculiarity is neglected or suppressed.
>
> . . . Since the universal factors always appear only in individual form, a full consideration of them will also produce an individual effect, and one which cannot be surpassed by anything else, least of all by individualism.[71]

> In general, [individuation] is the process by which individual beings are formed and differentiated; in particular, it is the development of the psychological individual as a being distinct from the general, collective psychology.[72]

> The aim of individuation is nothing less than to divest the self of the false wrappings of the persona on the one hand, and of the suggestive power of primordial images on the other.[73]

> As the individual is not just a single, separate being, but by his very existence presupposes a collective relationship, it follows that the process of individuation must lead to more intense and broader collective relationships and not to isolation.[74]

---

[71] "The Function of the Unconscious," CW 7, pars. 267f.
[72] Definitions, *Psychological Types,* par. 757.
[73] "The Function of the Unconscious," *Two Essays,* CW 7, par. 269.
[74] "Definitions," *Psychological Types,* CW 6, par. 758.

Individuation does not shut one out from the world, but gathers the world to oneself.[75]

In short, individualism is blatant me-first selfishness, alienated from any concern for others, whereas individuation is a process of psychological differentiation, having for its goal the development of the individual personality and how that might also contribute to—or fit in with—the collective. Jung again: "If a plant is to unfold its specific nature to the full, it must first be able to grow in the soil in which it is planted."[76]

Individuation is a process informed by the archetypal ideal of wholeness, which in turn depends on a vital relationship between ego and unconscious. The aim is not to overcome one's personal psychology, to become perfect, but to become familiar with it. Thus individuation involves an increasing awareness of one's unique psychological reality, including personal strengths and limitations, and at the same time a deeper appreciation of humanity in general. Jung expands on this:

> Individuation has two principle aspects: in the first place it is an internal and subjective process of integration, and in the second it is an equally indispensable process of objective relationship. Neither can exist without the other, although sometimes the one and sometimes the other predominates.[77]

Individuation and a life lived by collective values are nevertheless two divergent destinies. In Jung's view they are related to one another by guilt. Whoever embarks on the personal path becomes to some extent estranged from collective values, but does not thereby lose those aspects of the psyche which are inherently collective. To atone for this "desertion," the individual is obliged to create something of worth for the benefit of society.

> Individuation cuts one off from personal conformity and hence from collectivity. That is the guilt which the individuant leaves behind him for the

---

[75] "On the Nature of the Psyche," *The Structure and Dynamics of the Psyche,* CW 8, par. 432.

[76] "Definitions," CW 6, par. 760.

[77] "The Psychology of the Transference," CW 16, par. 448.

world, that is the guilt he must endeavor to redeem. He must offer a ransom in place of himself, that is, he must bring forth values which are an equivalent substitute for his absence in the collective personal sphere. Without this production of values, final individuation is immoral and—more than that—suicidal. . . .

The individuant has no *a priori* claim to any kind of esteem. He has to be content with whatever esteem flows to him from outside by virtue of the values he creates. Not only has society a right, it also has a duty to condemn the individuant if he fails to create equivalent values.[78]

To sum up, then, individuation deviates from collective norms but retains respect for them, while individualism eschews them entirely in favor of self-interest. Jung writes:

A real conflict with the collective norm arises only when an individual way is raised to a norm, which is the actual aim of extreme individualism. Naturally this aim is pathological and inimical to life. It has, accordingly, nothing to do with individuation, which, though it may strike out on an individual bypath, precisely on that account needs the norm for its orientation to society and for the vitally necessary relationship of the individual to society. Individuation, therefore, leads to a natural esteem for the collective norm.[79]

The process of individuation, consciously pursued, leads to the realization of the Self as a psychic reality greater than the ego. Thus individuation is essentially different from the process of simply becoming conscious. Jung again:

The goal of the individuation process is the synthesis of the self.[80]

Again and again I note that the individuation process is confused with the coming of the ego into consciousness and that the ego is in consequence identified with the self, which naturally produces a hopeless conceptual muddle. Individuation is then nothing but ego-centredness and autoeroticism. But the self comprises infinitely more than a mere ego, as the sym-

---

[78] "Adaptation, Individuation, Collectivity," *The Symbolic Life,* CW 18, pars. 1095f.
[79] "Definitions," *Psychological Types,* CW 6, par. 761.
[80] "The Psychology of the Child Archetype," CW 9i, par. 278.

bolism has shown from of old. It is as much one's self, and all other selves, as the ego.[81]

Of course, no one is ever completely individuated. While the goal is wholeness and a healthy working relationship with the Self—the regulating center of the psyche—the true value of individuation lies in what happens along the way. As Jung notes:

> The goal is important only as an idea; the essential thing is the *opus* which leads to the goal: *that* is the goal of a lifetime.[82]

I showed Adam what I'd written so far and asked him: "So, where does that leave us?"

"Not entirely in the dark," he said. "But gray is my natural habitat. Maybe that's why I like *film noir*."

I could not gainsay that, for I too was a fan of *film noir*. Think of Orson Wells in *The Third Man* or Bogey in Raymond Chandler's *The Big Sleep.*

And what does all that have to do with me? How does what I write about fit into my life? Those are relevant questions when you are seriously involved in your own process of individuation. Whatever affects you, what brings tears to your eyes, joy or grief, that is the essence of you that you had better get to know or it will go underground and may hurt those you love.

---

[81] "On the Nature of the Psyche," CW 8, par. 432.

[82] "The Psychology of the Transference," *The Practice of Psychotherapy,* CW 16, par. 400.

11
Looking Back

My first job out of university, in the fall of 1957, was with a large multinational corporation, namely Procter & Gamble. P & G recruited me from the journalism class at Carleton University in Ottawa. I had been president of the Students' Council and was a prime candidate for the corporate world—career oriented, conscientious, enthusiastic. The salary was $3,000 a year, pretty good at the time. My title was Director of Public Relations for Canada. Big deal! I was an unconscious, happy-go-lucky extravert. More: at the ripe young age of 21, I had status. I was cock of the walk. The world was my oyster.

"Security," said my P & G handlers, pointing out the company's many products: soap, toothpaste, cake-mix, nut-oil, strawberry conserve, beef sausages, fish fingers, oleo margarine, maple syrup, peanut butter, and so much more. "And don't forget," they said, "Procter is -er, damn it, not -or!"

They flew me down to Cleveland to meet the top brass.

"Personal hygiene and food," they said. "People always gotta eat. They may not wash but even in a depression people gotta eat."

The people in the company were all very friendly. We called each other by our first names and higher management ate with us in the staff canteen. We had bowling teams and played softball together. I felt wanted. I had a community where I felt at home.

One of my jobs was to placate irate customers and make them feel important. They put me in a room with my name on the door and gave me a personal secretary. All the letters of complaint came to me. There were quite a few. I sat in a swivel chair with my feet on the desk and dictated answers.

"Dear Gladys, take a letter."

Gladys was my secretary. She was rather plump and had a silver hoop on each ear. I liked her. She was clearly more experienced at the game than I was, but she didn't let on. She smiled at me and transcribed what I said. That was her role, after all; she had no other and she filled it well.

"Dear Mr. Bell. Thank you for your recent letter period. We are most surprised to learn that unlike many thousands of satisfied Whitey Toothpaste users comma your teeth have turned black period. Although many laboratory tests have proved the Whitey whiteness claims comma it is just possible that in your case the effect may not be as immediate as with others period.

"Or as bad."

Gladys giggled. Dear Gladys, she thought I was a hoot.

"New paragraph. Ahhh, nevertheless comma, true to our guarantee, we herewith refund your purchase price plus postage, along with two free giant-size Whiteys period. We hope that you will persevere comma proving for yourself that Whitey Toothpaste really does make teeth whiter period. Yours sincerely etc.

"There are more of those, Gladys. Send a copy to Quality Control, with a memo: Whose teeth are you using down there?

"Say Gladys, where's that report on skin eruptions? Call Dave Stephens at the *Times*. Tell him I've been called away on important business. Tell him, uh, the company's lawyers are looking into these complaints with a view to settling out of court in case their truth in substance is established, which we do not of course admit. Send another memo to Quality Control: What are you doing to the Bunny Flakes? The old man is on to this. It could be your skin next.

"Gladys, take a letter.

"Dear Mr. Appleby comma. We are sorry indeed to hear of the distress you experienced through the use of our product comma Mother Maxwell's Quick-Make Bicky-Mix period. I assure you it is not usual to find a mouse in it period. Our Bicky-Mix foreman attributes this to the playful nature of some of our more junior employees comma who will certainly be duly disciplined period.

"New paragraph. Under separate cover we are sending you one dozen packs of Mother Maxwell's Quick-Make Bicky-Mix comma of assorted kinds period. We hope you will continue to inform us of any irregularities in our products that come to your attention period.

"New paragraph. Quality Control comma Mr. Appleby comma is an everyday concern here period. Yours etc.

"Gladys, inform Shipping to stand by with more gift cartons. The little buggers are at it again."

That's the way it went. Sand in the talcum powder, mice in the cake mix, hair in the jam. Some days I thought I'd go mad.

Gladys would punch out the letters on a tape and run off a few dozen copies on an electric typewriter that made them look individually typed. That was part of the game. I didn't think twice about it. Bound to be some problems in a company that size. Somebody had to answer the letters.

I was making decent money and having a ball. They said I had the right stuff and would move up through the ranks. I lived in a large bachelor flat with modern furniture and a hi-fi set. I had a two-year-old Dodge and a hand-made suit that cost $220. My girlfriend said I looked very impressive in midnight blue. I got a haircut every Thursday and used Wild Root Cream-Oil to keep it neat. I was a big spender. On payday I had a shoeshine for a quarter. "Here," I'd say, adding a nickel, "keep the change."

One of my duties was to edit and produce the P & G bi-monthly in-house magazine called "Moonbeams." They gave me an expensive camera and let me loose. I interviewed retirees and wrote articles about them. I took pictures of factory workers and secretaries and flirted with the lovelies. After work I played softball and drank beer with the guys.

I was doing what my education had prepared me for. Others of my age were climbing mountains, exploring jungles, roaming around the world. I did not envy them. Why would I? They were shirking the duties of real life. They had no place in society, whereas I was a valuable member of the community.

I loved being a junior executive; it was a lot of fun. I could not think of anything I'd rather do—well, until I fell in with contrary companions—beatniks we called them in those days— who disdained the corporate ethic and encouraged me to aim higher. So I read *Organization*

Man—an anti-establishment bestseller in the '50s—and I began to feel restless for something else.

I talked to my friend Walt about it. Walt was a stringer for Reuter's wire service. He lived in a room in a college frat house because it was cheap. We'd studied journalism together. Walt had dreams of being a foreign correspondent in Karachi. Reuter's put him on something called pig stocks.

"Walt," I said, helping myself to a beer and some Cheese-Whiz, "I'm uneasy and I don't know why."

Walt reclined in a dentist's chair he'd picked up in a garage sale. He cradled a bottle and chewed gum with his mouth open. He was holding a copy of Submariner, a comic book he favored. A dusty fan ticked overhead. Dirty clothes were piled in a corner. Dishes were stacked in the sink and the radio didn't work. A display window dummy, dressed in pink pajamas, was propped against one wall. Dozens of egg cartons, painted bright yellow, had been stapled to the ceiling. Walt told me they were good insulation against noise. The yellow was for looks. The room was divided by a wooden trestle with the stenciled words, Caution—Men At Work.

I was not taken with Walt's way of life, but I was fascinated because he saw things in a way I didn't.

I made myself a sweet onion sandwich and downed a few olives. "I have a job that many guys would give their eye teeth for," I said. "I worked darn hard to get it. My family is proud of me. Why doesn't it feel right?"

Walt shrugged. Most of my peers envied me. They clapped me on the back and said I was a leader among men. But Walt was not impressed.

"Your life is taken up with cruddy minutiae," he said. "Your work has no meaning."

"I'm sure that what I do is a great help to many people," I said defensively. I was annoyed. Walt would borrow money from me but he didn't respect what I did to earn it. Sure, I could laugh about it with Gladys, but that was between us, in-house talk. I was actually very proud of my job.

Walt took a swig and scratched his belly. He was short and fat. His head was shaved bald. He wore a torn and stained t-shirt. With high cheekbones, thick sensuous lips and a jutting forehead, he looked a lot like Neanderthal man.

Walt was a slob, pure and simple. That was his persona; what you saw was what you got. He mocked organized society and tolerated no pretensions. He was forever exposing the banalities of polite conversation.

"Yes," I would agree, "The expression 'How are you?' means nothing. But it breaks the ice."

"I hear you," he'd say, fingering his pate. "But I prefer ice."

When he wasn't filing stories for Reuter's Walt hung out in The Black Bull, a tavern with seven pool tables. He played poker and shot craps with the locals. He drank a lot and fell down stairs. I could never understand why some women liked him. My girlfriend thought he was obnoxious. She refused to have anything to do with him after he stuck his finger in her ear.

Walt and I were as different as night and day. I lived on the surface, all show. Walt lived out of his gut, close to the ground. I was always a bit afraid of him because he didn't live by my rules, or in fact any rules at all. However, he took me to Ukrainian weddings, where I danced all night and went around saying, "Yaksamiyish!" I wasn't sure what that meant but it made me feel happy.

Once I took Walt to a luncheon meeting of the Industrial Editors' Association. I coached him beforehand on how to behave.

"Don't drink too much," I pleaded. "They know me here."

Walt was fine until the head speaker, already swaying after four martinis, suddenly stopped in mid-sentence, went all white, put a hand to his mouth and threw up between his fingers. Walt was uncontrollable after that.

I said to Walt: "P & G makes everything under the sun. Without it the world would be a sorrier place."

Walt belched. "And what would you be without P & G?"

I had no answer for that. Such a question had never occurred to me. I had been groomed for a world where the road to success was paved with ten million best-selling copies of Dale Carnegie's *How To Win Friends and Influence People.* That was my life and I knew no other. I won't say it's what I had in mind when I went into the world to make my mark, but all the same I had everything I wanted.

"I have everything I want," I said, chewing on a bunch of dried Chinese noodles.

That was one thing about Walt. He never cooked a decent meal but he always had great snack food.

"So why are you uneasy?" said Walt.

"That's what I asked you in the first place," I said, savoring a pickled kipper.

"I'm not your therapist," said Walt, "but what about those books you were going to write?"

I munched an oyster on a Ritz biscuit. Yes, I vaguely recalled dreams of being an author. Like almost everyone else in our class I had had fantasies of writing *The Great Canadian Novel.*

"That wasn't the real world," I said dismissively.

"Reality is what you make it," said Walt.

He heaved out of the dentist's chair and tossed his cigarette in the sink. "Look, go eat in a restaurant, I'm expecting a chick."

Walt's words haunted me.

I thought more about my earlier ambitions. I started reading again: Thomas Wolfe, Hemingway, Steinbeck, Scott Fitzgerald, Kerouac, Ferlinghetti, Ginsberg. I became more and more dissatisfied. I no longer enjoyed photo jaunts to the factory. I missed important meetings. I took long wet lunch breaks and left work early to play snooker with Walt. He taught me which color came next and how to put English on the cue ball. I took flute lessons instead of boning up on new brand names. My bowling average dropped.

I had a bad case of itchy feet. Although I didn't actually come to dislike the work I was doing day-to-day, it just became "meaningless" to me, and I fretted about that.

It finally came down to this: By September 1959 I had saved a thousand dollars. That was enough to buy a 1957 Thunderbird, or it would pay for a trip to Europe. How I lusted after that sporty car. But Europe! Holy Toledo! I read of writers who had lived in Paris on the Left Bank, and I longed for that bohemian life.

I finally eschewed the Thunderbird and bought a ticket on a freighter from Montreal to Le Havre on the coast of France: the *TSS (Twin Screw Steamer) New York.*

The young guys at work understood why I was leaving. Those who were firmly ensconced didn't. Jim Withers, the advertising manager, dropped into my office. He was a twenty-year man in his early fifties.

"Hear you're leaving us."

"That's right." I smiled. "Time to try something different."

"You've been here, what, two years now?"

"That's right."

"You won't get your profit-sharing bonuses."

I shrugged.

Jim went to the window, chewing the stub of a pencil. I knew what was coming next.

"You want more money, is that it?"

"No."

"You don't think there's a future here for you?"

"I'm sure there is, that's what I'm afraid of."

Mr. Withers was only the advance guard. Over the next few weeks they popped in and out, one after the other, offering condolences, paying their last respects.

"Always a place here for a bright boy."

"You were going places."

"You'll lose your pension rights."

They looked at me as if I had some loathsome disease. And who was to say it might not be catching? It reminded me of the way married couples react when they hear of partners who have split up. They close ranks, like mourners at a funeral, viewing the remains.

There were others. Relatives, friends of the family, neighbors, people I once knew at school. At odd hours they came, accosted me in the street. They sent little notes expressing dismay. They who hardly knew me.

"Come back and be one of us," they said.

They made it very hard to leave.

My boss took me out for lunch. We sat around his club smoking expensive cigars while he gave me a lecture on affluence—why not to be cynical about it.

"You'll always regret leaving, son," he said. "You'll never get a better job."

"You've been very understanding, Mr. Jones," I said earnestly.

I rather liked the old guy. He was a great talker, a born salesman. Ask him what time it was and he'd tell you how to make a watch. He could sell mousetraps to cats. His hair was steely gray and one leg was shorter than the other. He'd been with the company for thirty-five years and loved it.

"I'm still young," I said. "There's lots of time. I hope one day you'll be proud of me." That was a bald-faced lie, but what can you do, I was still a Dale Carnegie acolyte.

Before leaving I was asked to recommend someone for my position. I told them Walt would be an excellent choice.

"You think he's executive material?"

"He's just the man," I said with conviction.

I thought it was a huge joke, but Walt was offered the job. And to my surprise he took it.[83]

The *TSS New York* took two weeks to cross the Atlantic but I was in no hurry. I exulted in my new persona, the sense of myself as a struggling writer. On the boat I flirted shamelessly and became the ping-pong champ and the librarian, while between times I wrote and mimeographed the daily bulletin of events, the *TSS New Yorker,* which was my entrée into many a lovely's cabin before dawn or after dark. So on top of everything, I was a Don Juan in training. I was buoyant, full to overflowing with my new life.

I took a train from Le Havre directly to Paris and found a charming

---

[83] For the rather tragic aftermath, see my *Dear Gladys: The Survival Papers,* Book 2, pp. 51ff.

little hotel on the Left Bank, near *Les Deux Maggots,* where it was said that Henry Miller and Hemingway used to hang out. My room had mirrors on all the walls and on the ceiling too. I set up my typewriter and waited for inspiration. None came. I went to the museums, crossed all the bridges and dawdled along the Seine. I felt very lonely. I went out in the evening to pubs, cabarets, dance halls, and before long I picked up a cuddly mademoiselle, a professional translator who spoke seven languages. She kept me company in the mirrors for several months—well, until I ran out of money. She was delightful, but no fool.

Well, then I was up against it: go back to Canada and resume my interrupted career, or find some other way to survive. I had letters from my former boss at P & G saying they would welcome me back. On the other hand, I knew from friends that in England there was a desperate need for substitute teachers, and teacher training was not required. Also, at that time, anyone from the British Commonwealth was welcome to live and work in England. So a few days later I took off to London on the cross-channel ferry.

Oh, how can I express my delight with England? Sure, I had enjoyed Paris, but I fell head over heals in love with London! I was not psychologically minded in those days and I didn't record my dreams, but I knew how I felt. I was ecstatic; every day was a new epiphany. Theater, opera, dance, all that. After seeing a performance I got so excited wandering the foggy London streets that I often stood motionless, waiting for someone to appear, a giant perhaps, who'd shout, "STOP! Stop enjoying yourself! It's not allowed."

I shared a basement apartment with three other ex-patriot Canadians in the heart of Chelsea—20 Cadogan Gardens, near Sloane Square. We were a real mixed bag. There was Dick, a salesman with General Electric; Irving, a short and dumpy fan of Lewis Carroll and foreign correspondent for the *Calgary Herald;* Ralph, my long-standing friend from Carleton University; and me, a self-proclaimed struggling writer who inexplicably identified with those giants who exemplified the modern European mind: Kafka, Beckett, Kierkegaard, Nietzsche, Camus, Dostoyevsky and the poet Rilke. Well, in Jung-speak—as I later learned—that's called inflation, though I wouldn't have behaved any differently if I'd known it at the time. In short, I was a callow, hedonistic, self-indulgent youth masquerading as a wise old man, and enjoying myself no end.

I was making ends meet by teaching in Secondary Modern Schools, the bottom rung of the English education system. It wasn't hard to get work. Especially in Battersea and Wandsworth, where classroom riots were the norm and canes were standard issue. I vividly recall a room in chaos, with a mischievous little tyke peeking out from under a desk and pleading with me, "Hang in there, sir, we need you!"

My favorite evening pastime then was pub-walking with my mates along Fulham Road. First we'd have a pint in the Queen's Elm, then the Fox and Fiddle, and finally Finch's, the teeming Irish pub where there was always action: cool pints of Guinness, poets on pulpits and pussy willing.[84] It all happened in Finch's, according to *The Daily Mirror, The News of the World* and *The Evening Standard.* And they were right. I wallowed in the Dionysian scene and when I got home in the wee hours I wrote about it, wondering all the time about the close-knitness, the congruence, of body, soul and spirit. Those early notebooks comprise what I now call my juvenilia, which in later years I scavenged for material to use in my published books. Well, every writer does it.

Saturday night and Finch's is packed. Familiar faces of stage and screen loll against the wall. Long-faced girls, living Modigliani prints, perch on stools. Thick black eyelashes. Purple make-up. Looping Gypsy earrings. Floppy woolen sweaters. If you see it in Finch's, it's in—or soon will be.

The air is thick with smoke and husky voices.

"Horses, my dear, are absolutely out."

"Will it sell he said, Christ as if I cared."

---

[84] I don't mean to suggest that Finch's was frequented by low-life broads, but rather canny ones, for as I have already said, I believe that the way to a man's heart is not through his stomach but through his groin. The women who realize this become courtesans, paramours, wives. A man's attendant responsibilities are well detailed in Monick, *Potency,* pp. 21ff.

"Do let me bring Akhbar, he's ever so much fun."

Irving sits in a corner miming "The Jabberwock." Ralph stands on a table, loudly reciting lines from Rilke: "Now to depart from all this incoherence that's ours, / but which we can't appropriate . . . / O fountain mouth, you mouth that can respond so inexhaustibly to all who ask . . ."—and one of my favorites: "Who if I cried would hear me among the angelic orders?"

On my right two smart dressers on a crawl through fashionable Chelsea are being worked over by men in beards. On my left, an American girl in horn-rimmed glasses is pumping the hand of an Indian boy. "Gee, fancy meeting you here."

Dick and Irving approach with a girl in tow.

"This is Wendy," says Dick. "I found a toad feeling her up in the corner. I squashed him."

Dick disappears. While Irving licks Wendy's ear I flirt with her eyes. She is Irish, elf-like, four foot ten, nicely curved. Wendy is a waitress in a restaurant up the street. She's just finished her shift and is loaded for bear. Her eyes twinkle.

"Do you come here often?" I ask.

Wendy smiles and rubs her leg against Irving. She rummages in a large satchel for a pack of smokes.

"I was once goosed by Brendan Behan," she says.

Wendy was real cute and had a wicked sense of humor. I wasn't at all surprised when Irving married her and took her home to Alberta to make babies.

Well, I found teaching in London just too stressful, so after a year I went back to Toronto and accepted a job with Canadian Press. It was exciting at first. I got to go to all kinds of political and social functions and write a few paragraphs about them. But after a few months I was bored to tears. It was all so superficial. Again, what I was doing had no meaning. I finished writing a book—*Notebooks of a Prodigal Son*—and sent it off to publishers but it was always rejected. Good thing too—it was a narcissistic disaster.

As it happened, at that time I had a friend whose father owned a cargo plane. He had a contract to fly rhesus monkeys from India to Canada for use in medical research. My friend said he could get me on a flight to England, where the plane stopped in Birmingham on the way back to India. And so, one dark October night, as rain fell in Moncton, New Brunswick, I slung my bag into the hold of a decrepit DC-3.

The flight took twenty-four hours. We droned over the Atlantic at 6,000 feet. There were two bucket-seats for passengers and a lot of empty cages. An Indian fellow named Roger sat beside me. He was the company agent. Every few hours he took a bag of sandwiches from his battered suitcase and shared them out.

"Hey boy," said Roger. He'd done this run many times. "You don't want to be on this kite when it's loaded with monkeys."

"Oh?" I was watching the ocean liners far below. They would take five or six days or more.

"Monkeys don't like heights," said Roger. "They shit and piss and throw up."

"I can imagine."

The sensation of being free was very strong that night. My heart was full. I was really looking forward to getting back to London.

"You got no idea," said Roger. "Once we hit an air pocket and the plane dropped 500 feet. All that shit and monkey vomit spilled out of the cages and there I was in the middle of it. I tell you I was sick, boy."

"That must have been awful," I said.

I didn't know what was in store for me, but I wasn't sorry to be on the move again.

"Sheer terror," said Roger.

The guys welcomed me back to the basement apartment in Chelsea and I resumed my footloose life as an unpublished struggling writer.

Everything was hunky-dory until I fell crazy in love with Brenda, my friend Ralph's girlfriend. That made life in Cadogan Gardens awkward, so Brenda and I debouched to the south of France on her Lambretta and camped out for some months on a hill in Sète in the Languedoc region. Now that sure was an idyllic time. We explored Europe on her scooter and lived in youth hostels. We made love everywhere and forever and before long, surprise, Brenda was pregnant. She was not pleased, but I was because, as I said to her, it was a powerful reason for us to get married, which we did, and Ralph graciously agreed to be my best man. Well, this was 1960, when abortions and common-law unions with children weren't usual. Thereafter we had a loving relationship for twelve years and three wonderful children to show for it.

It was only much later, in retrospect, that I realized that my desire to marry Brenda was rooted in a possessive fantasy—that she would then become my property, indeed my sex slave, and unavailable to other men. Well, that's a patriarchal attitude, for sure, and I'm not entirely quit of it. But meanwhile, during our mutual struggles, Brenda and I parted ways and I firmly launched myself on a path of self-discovery that took me into Jungian analysis and the arms of other women.

No doubt about it, after leaving Brenda my Don Juan shadow took over. I courted many women and bedded more than a few. The *American Heritage Dictionary* defines a Don Juan as "1) libertine, profligate; 2) a man obsessed with seducing women."

Well, I guess I was all that, but as a matter of fact, at the time I thought of my erotic pursuits in terms of accumulating experience of women so as to become more familiar with the feminine in myself—my so-called anima, you see—which, I thought, would contribute to my process of individuation that in Jung-speak is the Golden Grail of life.

Talk about self-serving head stuff. But what can I say, I didn't know anything about my shadow then. And I certainly didn't reckon on the impact that my phallic intrusion into a woman's life might have. I soon learned, though, courtesy in no small part to a woman biting my ear in a Zurich pub, when I thought she was just wanting to whisper sweet nothings. . . . Well, that's how unconscious I was. My ear needed six stitches, my psyche many more.

So, where is this going? Well, maybe nowhere, but listen, the goal is a chimera; you never get there anyway, and if by some very unlikely, remote chance you do, everything's different by then—so you might as well sit back, read Franz Kafka on the absurdity of life and enjoy the journey.

12
The Wonderful World of Women

I like women. I like everything about them—the way they walk, the way they talk, their clothes, their smell, their taste, their bodies. I never met a cleavage I didn't fancy.

Fortunately I am blessed with the ability to focus, and so, although I may have rich fantasies, I can usually limit my behavior to the lovely right in front of me. I'm not saying that is the only way for one to be, or even the best, only that I can do no other. Indeed, I think there is nothing so exciting as making love with the responsive one right in front of you. Which is to say, when I'm in love I am monogamous.

All the same, perhaps paradoxically—and welcome to the world of opposites—I can hardly meet a woman without measuring the possibility of having sex with her.[85] Hey, think of it. Western culture, in advertising, films, television and the world of fashion, promotes women as sex objects. I would like to think I'm immune to all that, but of course I'm not, nor are my hormones. Women may complain, but see how they collude. Just consider the bare mid-riff look and the incredibly sexy backpack strap crossing the breasts. What with bouncing bosoms, short-shorts, mini-skirts and loose or tight-fitting jeans, men are teased to the brink. Talk about provocation! Only a eunuch could walk a block without getting an erection.

Anyway, enough of that prurient talk. I am thinking now of when I courted MP, my paramour. I romanced her in many ways. I sent her poetry, I gave her flowers; I took her to concerts; we walked and shopped together. I fell madly in love and she finally responded with her own erotic vitality. Oh, joyful wisdom! Beyond good and evil! Now I give her lingerie and deliver incendiary *billets doux* by courier. When she comes to tryst and shout I play Rod Stewart and mime the words:

---

[85] I reckon many men could say the same, though loath to admit it, but I'm not about to do a survey.

It's very clear, our love is here to stay
Not for a year but ever and a day
The radio and the telephone and the movies that we know
May just be passing fancies and in time may go
But oh my dear, our love is here to stay.[86]

Yes, it is true that I have been a feckless Don Juan and an inveterate flirt, but no more. My feeling for MP anchors me; her love thrills me through and through. To hold her close is a numinous experience, nay, transcendent—by which I mean it takes me utterly out of myself and onto an entirely different plane that might as well be called holy.

"I feel safe in you," I say to her.

"I feel sheltered in your arms," she replies.

I confided this exchange to Nurse Pam, who said: "Yes, you are very safe with MP and with me, your very own loverNot . . . a double Brinks. . . . I feel the same with you. The safety is in our individual centered-ness—where the arrow-projections for the most part are shot by cupids and not devils. Not that we're anywhere near perfect, but we know that we aren't, and we have an eye out for which god might be slinging the arrows."

Was it not ever thus between man and woman? Each contains the other. Romantic notion? Yes, for sure! But that's the whole point. At the age of sixty-nine you might think I'd get over it, but no, I still feel that romantic love is the best it gets. Nothing can touch the magic or the mystery of it, not even the rush of creativity. I have known life without requited passion, and it is dross: drab, colorless, boring. Just ask Frank Sinatra, who claimed he didn't understand women, and then listen to him massaging a ballad, for instance:

A voice within me keeps repeating
Night and day,
You are the one.
Only you beneath the moon or under the sun.

---

[86] "Our Love Is Here to Stay," on *As Time Goes By: The Great American Songbook, vol. II.* Lyrics by George and Ira Gershwin.

> Whether near to me or far,
> No matter, darling,
> I think of you,
> Night and day.[87]

Or this:

> We may have been meant for each other,
> To be or not to be, let our hearts discover . . .
> But I adore you, so strong for you.
> Let's fall in love,
> Why shouldn't we fall in love?
> Our hearts are made of it,
> Why be afraid of it?
> Let's close our eyes and make our own paradise . . .
> Let's fall in love.[88]

And this! —

> Lately, I find myself
> Out gazing at stars,
> Hearing guitars,
> Like someone in love.
> Sometimes the things I do astound me,
> Mostly whenever you're around me.
> Lately I seem to walk as though I had wings,
> I bump into things
> Like someone in love.
> Each time I look at you,
> I'm limp as a glove
> And feeling like someone in love.[89]

Okay, so all that doesn't prove anything. But what is there to prove? A relationship isn't a scientific experiment, where you end up with a foreseen result—Q.E.D, it's called in Latin: *quod erat demonstrandum* (that

[87] "Night and Day," on *Frank Sinatra: Romance*. Lyrics by Cole Porter.
[88] "Let's Fall in Love," ibid. Lyrics by Harold Arlen and Ted Koehler.
[89] "Like Someone in Love," ibid. Lyrics by Jimmy van Heusen and Johnny Burke.

which was to be proved). That was an important tenet in my early education, and for years I took that principle into life, but in the end it just didn't work, and so no more. Logos has long since given way in my life to eros. I no longer have to prove anything. I just have to honor how I feel, which as it happens is not really easier than proving a hypothesis in physics. But I can tell you, it sure is a lot more satisfying.

All right, back now to my sweetheart MP and Nurse Pam, my lover-Not. Well, I would feel lost without either of them; that says something. Of course, I have my inner woman too, dear Rachel, but she is diaphanous and doesn't massage my feet.

I find it invigorating to have relationships with two real women. I bask in the feeling of requited desire, whether acted on or not.

Of course there is a shadow side, as there is to everything—some guilt and anxiety because our connections are covert. But Nurse Pam and MP, on the whole, and how I admire them for it, are able to hold the tension between their feelings for me and their fealty to their spouses. Lucky me—and them too, they say. Here is the incomparable Sarah Vaughan on that very theme:

> Time after time, I tell myself that I'm
> So lucky to be loving you.
> So lucky to be the one you run to see
> In the evening, when the day is through.
>
> I only know what I know, the passing years will show
> You've kept my love so young, so new.
> And time after time, you'll hear me say that I'm
> So lucky to be loving you.[90]

And yet, and yet. A few days ago I woke up to the thought that all I really want is for a woman to make me cucumber sandwiches and welcome me in bed. . . . So, meet my chauvinist pig shadow. I'm not proud of him, nor, I imagine, is he of me. But we are joined at the hip, so we live with the tension and get along as best we can.

---

[90] "Time After Time," on *Sarah Vaughan: Young Sassy,* "Tenderly" (Disc Two). Lyrics by Sammy Cahn and Jule Styne.

13
Holding the Tension

Holding the tension between opposites is a central concept in the school of analytical psychology, as it is with anyone who works therapeutically in Jung's name.

What is involved in the tension between opposites? Why is it important and how does it work?

Well, let us start with conflict.

Any conflict situation constellates the problem of opposites. Broadly speaking, "the opposites" refers to the ego and the unconscious. This is true whether the conflict is recognized as an internal one or not, since conflicts with other people are almost always externalizations of an unconscious conflict within oneself. Because they are not made conscious, they are acted out on others. This is a subset of projection, discussed earlier. Here let us look more closely at the psychology of conflict.

Whatever attitude exists in consciousness, the opposite is in the unconscious. There is no way to haul this out by force. If we try, it will refuse to come. That is why the process of analysis is apt to be unproductive unless there is an active conflict. Indeed, as long as outer life proceeds relatively smoothly and with meaning, there is no need to deal with the unconscious. But when it doesn't, there is no way to avoid it.

The classic conflict situation is one in which there is the possibility of, or temptation to, more than one course of action. Theoretically the options may be many. But in practice a conflict is usually between two, each carrying its own chain of consequences. In such cases the psychological reality is that two separate personalities are involved. These may be thought of as different aspects of oneself; in other words, as personifications of complexes. Think about that for a minute—what a revolutionary idea........

Perhaps the most painful conflicts of all are those involving duty or a choice between security and freedom. Such conflicts generate a great deal of inner tension. As long as they are not conscious, the tension manifests as physical symptoms, particularly in the stomach, the back and the neck. Conscious conflict, on the other hand, is experienced as moral or ethical tension between, for instance, what we personally deem to be "right" and "wrong."

I have worked analytically with married men and women who had covert love affairs and troubling physical ailments. By and large, they came to me because of job-related problems or a pervasive sense of meaninglessness—not because they had a conflict over their love life. Their physical symptoms often vanished when their right hand (ego) openly acknowledged what their left hand (shadow) was doing. There followed moral tension and a conscious search for resolution.

Conflict is a hallmark of neurosis, but conflict is not invariably neurotic. Life naturally involves the collision between conflicting obligations and incompatible desires. Some degree of conflict is even desirable, since without it the flow of life is sluggish. Conflict only becomes neurotic when it settles in and interferes with the way one functions.

As mentioned earlier, I used to imagine that somewhere there was a big book of collective wisdom called something like *What To Do When.* It contained the prescribed solution to all life's problems. Whenever you found yourself in a conflict you could just look it up in the book and do what it said.

When I talked to Professor Brillig about this he pointed out that such a fantasy comes from the father complex. If there were a book like that, he said, I wouldn't have to think for myself—I'd just do what was laid down by tradition. How true—and how far from what is meant by individuation.

You see, individual problems have only individual solutions.

Two preliminary possibilities exist for resolving a conflict. You can tally up the pro's and con's on each side and reach a logically satisfying decision, or you can opt for what you "really want," then proceed to do what is necessary to make it possible.

Many minor conflicts are amenable to reason, and those that can be decided by reason without injurious effects can safely be left to reason. But serious conflicts do not so easily disappear; in fact they often arise precisely because of a one-sided rational attitude, and thus are more likely to be prolonged than solved by reason alone.

Where this is so, it is appropriate to ask, "But what do *I* want?"—or alternatively, "What do I *want?*" Of course, if one were sure of what one wanted, one would probably not have a conflict in the first place. But from a psychological point of view these are still useful questions, for the first, with the accent on "I," clarifies the individual ego position (as opposed to what others might want of you), and the second, stressing "want," activates the feeling function (judgment, evaluation).

A really serious conflict invariably involves a disparity between the typological functions of thinking and feeling. If feeling is not a conscious participant in the conflict, it needs to be introduced, and the same can be said for thinking.

It may happen that the ego position coincides with, or can accept, the attitude based on feeling. But if these are not compatible and the ego refuses to give way, then the situation remains at an impasse. That is the clinical picture of neurotic conflict, the resolution of which requires a dialogue with one's other sides. We can learn a good deal about ourselves through relationships with others, but the unconscious is a more objective mirror of who we really are.

Jung, commenting on the psychology of conflict, was fond of referring to the Biblical parable of Buridan's ass, the donkey that starved to death between two piles of hay because he couldn't make a choice. Jung pointed out that the important thing was not whether the bundle on the right or the one on the left was the better, or which one he ought to eat first, but what he wanted in the depths of his being—which did he feel pushed toward?[91] In other words, one of my mantras: where did his energy want to go? Jung says it in a slightly different way: "What is it, at this moment and in this individual, that represents the natural urge of life? That is the question."[92] The dumb-ass died without knowing, as do many human dumb-asses.

Jung also believed that the potential resolution of a conflict is constel-

---

91 "The Structure of the Unconscious," *Two Essays,* CW 7, par. 487.
92 Ibid., par. 488.

lated by holding the tension between the opposites. When every motive has an equally strong countermotive—that is, when the conflict between consciousness and the unconscious is at its peak—there is a damming up of vital energy. But the psyche cannot tolerate a standstill. If the ego can hold the tension, something quite unexpected may emerge, an irrational "third," that effectively resolves the situation.

This is what Jung called the transcendent function, which typically manifests as a symbol. Here is how he described the process:

> [A conflict] requires a real solution and necessitates a third thing in which the opposites can unite. Here the logic of the intellect usually fails, for in a logical antithesis there is no third. The "solvent" can only be of an irrational nature. In nature the resolution of opposites is always an energic process: she acts *symbolically* in the truest sense of the word, doing something that expresses both sides, just as a waterfall visibly mediates between above and below.[93]

Outer circumstances may remain the same, but a change takes place in the individual. This change appears as a new attitude toward oneself and others; energy previously locked up in a state of indecision is released and once again it becomes possible to move forward. I believe this because I have experienced it.

At that point, it is as if you were to stand on a mountaintop watching a raging storm below—the storm may go on, but you are outside of it, to some extent objective, no longer emotionally stressed. There is a sense of peace. This is not essentially different from the traditional Christian concept of grace—"the peace that passeth understanding"—except that it doesn't come from a God in heaven; it wells up inside.

This process requires patience and a strong ego, otherwise a decision will be made out of desperation, just to escape the tension. But when a decision is made prematurely—that is, when the tension has not been held long enough—then the other side, the option that was not chosen, will be constellated even more strongly and you're right back in the fire.

To the objection that many conflicts are intrinsically insoluble, Jung

---

[93] "The Conjunction," *Mysterium Coniunctionis,* CW 14, par. 705.

replied that people sometimes take this view because they think only of external solutions, which often as not are simply evasions or rationalizations of the underlying problem. He believed that a real solution comes only from a change in attitude:

> If a man cannot get on with his wife, he naturally thinks the conflict would be solved if he married someone else. When such marriages are examined they are seen to be no solution whatever. The old Adam enters upon the new marriage and bungles it just as badly as he did the earlier one. A real solution comes only from within, and then only because the patient has been brought to a different attitude.[94]

In alchemical writings there is a famous precept known as the Axiom of Maria. It goes like this:

> One becomes two, two becomes three, and out of the third comes the one as the fourth.[95]

Jung saw this dictum as an apt metaphor for the process of individuation, a progressive advance of consciousness in which conflict plays a profoundly important part. In brief, *one* stands for the original, paradisiacal state of unconscious wholeness (e.g., childhood); *two* signifies the conflict between opposites (e.g., persona and shadow); *three* points to a potential resolution; *the third* is the transcendent function; and *the one as the fourth* is alchemical code for the Philosophers' Stone—psychologically equivalent to a transformed state of consciousness, a state of relative wholeness.

Thus simply put, individuation is a kind of circular odyssey, a spiral journey, where the aim is to get back to where you started, but knowing where you've been and what for.

The tension involved in the conflict between ego and shadow is commonly experienced as a kind of crucifixion. Surely it is no accident that the image of a man nailed to a cross has been an important symbol in Western civilization for two thousand years. Crucifixion symbolizes the

---

94 "Some Crucial Points in Psychoanalysis," *Freud and Psychoanalysis*, CW 4, par. 606.
95 *Psychology and Alchemy*, CW 12, par. 26

suffering involved in growing up, the difficult process of differentiating opposites and learning to live with them.

Franz Kafka pictured this literally, as a man tied to poles that could tear him apart. He sent this unsettling image in a letter to his sweetheart:

So that you can see something of my "occupations," I'm enclosing a drawing. There are four poles, through the two middle ones are driven rods to which the hands of the "delinquent" are fastened; through the two outer poles rods are driven for the feet. After the man has been bound in this way the rods are slowly drawn outwards until the man is torn apart in the middle.[96]

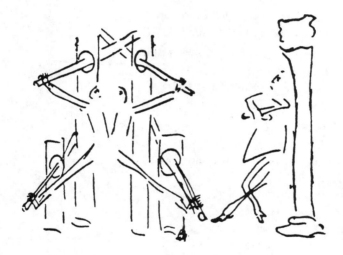

---

[96] See Kafka, *Letters to Milena*, p. 204; also Sharp, *The Secret Raven: Conflict and Transformation in the Life of Franz Kafka*, pp. 41f.

14
The Time of Your Life

Time passes, yes, but where does it go? This question has haunted me for the past few days. Next week I will turn seventy. It seems like only yesterday that I was a brash young executive bopping around with a camera for Procter and Gamble ("It's -er, damn it!"). And that was fifty years ago . . . I wonder: if I had stayed, would I be CEO by now or in a home for the terminally bereft?

Nina Simone sings some ideas on the subject of time:

> Across the morning sky, all the birds are leaving.
> How can they know when it's time to go?
>
> Before the winter fire, I will still be dreaming
> I do not count the time,
> for who knows where the time goes?
> Who knows where the time goes?
>
> Sad, deserted shore,
> your fickle friends are leaving.
> Oh, but then you know it was time for them to go.
> But I will still be here,
> I have no thought of leaving.
> I do not count the time
> for who knows where the time goes?
> Who knows where the time goes?
>
> I know I'm not alone
> while my love is near me.
> I know that it's so until it's time to go.
> All through the Winter and the through the birds in Spring again
> I do not count the time,
> for who knows where the time goes?
> Who knows where the time goes?[97]

---

[97] "Who Knows Where the Time Goes," on *Nina Simone: Love Songs.* Lyrics by Sandy Denny. Irving Music Inc. (BMI).

Well, I can't say better than that.

The writing of this book, slim as it is, has engaged me for more than a year. I say this not with pride, or looking for sympathy, but rather to encourage you to write your own story, no matter how long it takes, no matter that it might never be published. The important thing is to pay attention to both your inner and outer relationships—past, present, future. Focus on eros and do what is right in front of you. Above all, don't stop romancing the ones you love.

That, after all, is what gives life meaning and will keep you awake.

The Replica of Willendorf/post-prehistoric.
Jerry Pethick, Hornby Island, British Columbia, Canada. See page 4.
Installation view. Photo by Jim Gorman, Vancouver Art Gallery.

Bibliography

Campbell, Joseph. *The Hero with a Thousand Faces* (Bollingen Series XVII). Princeton: Princeton University Press, 1949.

Harding, M. Esther. *The I and the Not-I: A Study in the Development of Consciousness* (Bollingen Series LXXIX). Princeton: Princeton University Press, 1973.

_____. *The Parental Image: Its Injury and Reconstruction.* Toronto: Inner City Books, 2003.

_____. *The Way of All Women: A Psychological Interpretation.* London, UK: Rider and Company, 1971.

Hillman, James. *Insearch.* New York: Charles Scribner's Sons, 1967.

_____. *Loose Ends.* Zurich: Spring Publications, 1975.

Jacoby, Mario. *The Analytic Encounter: Trsnsference and Human Relationship.* Toronto: Inner City Books, 1984.

Jung, C.G. *The Collected Works* (Bollingen Series XX). 20 vols. Trans. R.F.C. Hull. Ed. H. Read, M. Fordham, G. Adler, Wm. McGuire. Princeton: Princeton University Press, 1953-1979.

_____. *Man and His Symbols.* London, UK: Aldus Books, 1964..

_____. *Memories, Dreams, Reflections.* Ed. Aniela Jaffé. New York: Pantheon Books, 1961.

_____. *The Psychology of Kundalini Yoga: Notes of the Seminar Given in 1932* (Bollingen Series XCIX). Ed. Sonu Shamdasani. Princeton: Princeton University Press, 1996.

Kafka, Franz. *The Diaries of Franz Kafka, 1910-1913.* Trans. Joseph Kresh. Ed. Max Brod. London: Martin Secker and Warburg, 1948.

_____. *Letters to Milena.* Ed. Willi Haas. Trans. Tania and James Stern. New York: Schocken Books, 1962.

_____. *The Penal Colony: Stories and Short Pieces.* Trans. Willa and Edwin Muir. New York: Schocken Books, 1961.

Leach, Maria, ed. *Funk & Wagnalls Standard Dictionary of Folklore, Mythology and Legend* (one volume edition). New York: Funk & Wagnalls, 1972.

McGuire, William, and Hull, R.F.C., eds. *C.G. Jung Speaking: Interviews and Encounters* (Bollingen Series XCVII). Princeton: Princeton University Press, 1977.

Meier, C.A. *Ancient Incubation and Modern Psychotherapy.* Evanston, IL: Northwestern University Press, 1967.

Monick, Eugene. *Phallos: Sacred Image of the Masculine.* Toronto: Inner City Books, 1987.

_____. *Potency: Masculine Aggression as a Path to the Soul.* Toronto: Inner City Books, 2006.

Rilke, Rainer Maria. *The Notebooks of Malte Laurids Brigge.* Trans. John Linton. London: The Hogarth Press, 1959.

Rumi, *The Essential Rumi.* Trans. Coleman Barks. New York: HarperSanFrancisco, 2004.

Sharp, Daryl. *Dear Gladys: The Survival Papers, Bk. 2.* Toronto: Inner City Books, 1989.

_____. *Jung Lexicon: A Primer of Terms and Concepts.* Toronto: Inner City Books, 1991.

_____. *Jungian Psychology Unplugged: My Life as an Elephant.* Toronto: Inner City Books, 1998.

_____. *Not the Big Sleep:On having fun, seriously (a Jungian romance).* Toronto: Inner City Books, 2005.

_____. *Personality Types: Jung's Model of Typology.* Toronto: Inner City Books, 1987.

_____. *The Secret Raven: Conflict and Transformation in the Life of Franz Kafka.* Toronto: Inner City Books, 1980.

_____. *The Survival Papers: Anatomy of a Midlife Crisis.* Toronto: Inner City Books, 1988.

_____. *Who Am I, Really? Personality, Soul and Individuation.* Toronto: Inner City Books, 1995.

Von Franz, Marie-Louise. *Alchemy: An Introduction to the Symbolism and the Psychology.* Toronto: Inner City Books, 1980.

_____. *The Problem of the Puer Aeternus.* 3rd edition. Toronto: Inner City Books, 2000.

Index

Page numbers in *italics* refer to illustrations

Procter & Gamble, 93-95, 97, 99-100,
116
project/projection, 14-15, 17, 26, 32,
37, 40, 44-46, 85, 110
psyche, 29, 37
self-regulation of, 36

questions, 112

Rachel, 25, 27, 31, 37, 79, 81, 83-85,
87
relationship(s), 15-16, 50-51, 53, 84,
108-109
Rilke, Rainer Maria: *The Notebooks of
Malte Laurids Brigge,* 3028ff

Scarab beetle, 87
schizophrenia, 61
Self, 81, 86, 91-92
self-regulation of the psyche, 36
sensation function/types, 51-55
shadow, 42, 52, 57, 63-67, 87, 105,
109, 111, 114
Simone, Nina, 116
Sinatra, Frank, 47, 51-52
soul, 38, 43
loss of, 41
spectrum, *59*
Sting: 74
subject and object, 54, 57
suicide, 28
sun, 72
superior function, 64. *See also*
typological/typology
tension between opposites, 68, 110-
113

therapy, 15-16, 28
thinking function/types, 53-55, 112
time, 116-117
"Time After Time," 109
transcendent function, 113-114
transference, 26, 32-33
treasure, in fairy tales, 70
typological/typology, 53-57, 62
tests of, 52, 55

unconscious, 14-15, 21-22, 28, 31-34,
37, 42-44, 51, 59-61, 63, 69, 82,
84, 86, 90, 110, 112-114
union of opposites, 52

visions, 29
von Franz, M.-L., 62
Alchemy, 86
Jung's Typology, 67
The Problem of the Puer Aeternus,
82

Walt, 96-98
"Who Knows Where the Time Goes,"
116
will power, 47, 54n
witches, 76-77
women, 106-109
and men, 50, 107
Word Association Experiment, 59-60
wounded healer, 32, *33,* 34

"You and the Night and the Music,"
51
"You Are," 62

Also by Daryl Sharp in this Series

Prices and Payment in $US (except in Canada, $Cdn)

THE SECRET RAVEN
Conflict and Transformation in the Life of Franz Kafka
ISBN 0-919123-00-7. (1980) 128 pp. $18

PERSONALITY TYPES: Jung's Model of Typology
ISBN 0-919123-30-9. (1987) 128 pp. Diagrams $18

THE SURVIVAL PAPERS: Anatomy of a Midlife Crisis
ISBN 0-919123-34-1. (1988) 160 pp. $18

DEAR GLADYS: The Survival Papers, Book 2
ISBN 0-919123-36-8. (1989) 144 pp. $18

JUNG LEXICON: A Primer of Terms and Concepts
ISBN 0-919123-48-1. (1991) 160 pp. Diagrams $18

GETTING TO KNOW YOU: The Inside Out of Relationship
ISBN 0-919123-56-2. (1992) 128 pp. $18

THE BRILLIG TRILOGY:

  1. CHICKEN LITTLE: The Inside Story *(A Jungian Romance)*
  ISBN 0-919123-62-7. (1993) 128 pp. $18

  2. WHO AM I, REALLY? Personality, Soul and Individuation
  ISBN 0-919123-68-6. (1995) 144 pp. $18

  3. LIVING JUNG: The Good and the Better
  ISBN 0-919123-73-2. (1996) 128 pp. $18

JUNGIAN PSYCHOLOGY UNPLUGGED: My Life as an Elephant
ISBN 0-919123-81-3. (1998) 160 pp. $18

CUMULATIVE INDEX of Inner City Books: The First 80 Titles, 1980-1998
ISBN 0-919123-82-1. (1999) 160 pp. 8-1/2" x 11" $20

DIGESTING JUNG: Food for the Journey
ISBN 0-919123-96-1. (2001) 128 pp. $18

NOT THE BIG SLEEP: On having fun, seriously *(A Jungian Romance)*
ISBN 0-919123-13-3. (2005) 128 pp. $18

Discounts: any 3-5 books, 10%; 6-9 books, 20%; 10 or more, 25%
Add Postage/Handling: 1-2 books, $6 surface ($10 air); 3-4 books, $8 surface ($12 air);
5-9 books, $15 surface ($20 air); 10 or more, $10 surface ($25 air)

Ask for **Jung at Heart** newsletter and complete Catalogue of **over 100 titles**

INNER CITY BOOKS
Box 1271, Station Q, Toronto, ON M4T 2P4, Canada
Tel. (416) 927-0355 / Fax (416) 924-1814 / E-mail: sales@innercitybooks.net

Studies in Jungian Psychology
by Jungian Analysts

Quality Paperbacks

Prices and payment in $US (except in Canada, $Cdn)

1. The Secret Raven: Conflict and Transformation
Daryl Sharp (Toronto). ISBN 0-919123-00-7. 128 pp. $18

2. The Psychological Meaning of Redemption Motifs in Fairy Tales
Marie-Louise von Franz (Zürich). ISBN 0-919123-01-5. 128 pp. $18

3. On Divination and Synchronicity: The Psychology of Meaningful Chance
Marie-Louise von Franz (Zürich). ISBN 0-919123-02-3. 128 pp. $18

4. The Owl Was a Baker's Daughter: Obesity, Anorexia and the Repressed Feminine Marion Woodman (Toronto). ISBN 0-919123-03-1. 144 pp. $18

5. Alchemy: An Introduction to the Symbolism and the Psychology
Marie-Louise von Franz (Zürich). ISBN 0-919123-04-X. 288 pp. $25

6. Descent to the Goddess: A Way of Initiation for Women
Sylvia Brinton Perera (New York). ISBN 0-919123-05-8. 112 pp. $18

8. Border Crossings: Carlos Castaneda's Path of Knowledge
Donald Lee Williams (Boulder). ISBN 0-919123-07-4. 160 pp. $18

9. Narcissism and Character Transformation: The Psychology of Narcissistic Character Disorders
Nathan Schwartz-Salant (New York). ISBN 0-919123-08-2. 192 pp. $20

11. Alcoholism and Women: The Background and the Psychology
Jan Bauer (Montreal). ISBN 0-919123-10-4. 144 pp. $18

12. Addiction to Perfection: The Still Unravished Bride
Marion Woodman (Toronto). ISBN 0-919123-11-2. 208 pp. $$20

13. Jungian Dream Interpretation: A Handbook of Theory and Practice
James A. Hall, M.D. (Dallas). ISBN 0-919123-12-0. 128 pp. $18

14. The Creation of Consciousness: Jung's Myth for Modern Man
Edward F. Edinger (Los Angeles). ISBN 0-919123-13-9. 128 pp. $18

15. The Analytic Encounter: Transference and Human Relationship
Mario Jacoby (Zürich). ISBN 0-919123-14-7. 128 pp. $18

17. The Illness That We Are: A Jungian Critique of Christianity
John P. Dourley (Ottawa). ISBN 0-919123-16-3. 128 pp. $18

19. Cultural Attitudes in Psychological Perspective
Joseph L. Henderson, M.D. (San Francisco). ISBN 0-919123-18-X. 128 pp. $18

21. The Pregnant Virgin: A Process of Psychological Transformation
Marion Woodman (Toronto). ISBN 0-919123-20-1. 208 pp. $20pb/$25hc

22. Encounter with the Self: A Jungian Commentary on William Blake's *Illustrations of the Book of Job*
Edward F. Edinger (Los Angeles). ISBN 0-919123-21-X. 80 pp. $18

23. The Scapegoat Complex: Toward a Mythology of Shadow and Guilt
Sylvia Brinton Perera (New York). ISBN 0-919123-22-8. 128 pp. $18

24. The Bible and the Psyche: Individuation Symbolism in the Old Testament
Edward F. Edinger (Los Angeles). ISBN 0-919123-23-6. 176 pp. $20

26. The Jungian Experience: Analysis and Individuation
James A. Hall, M.D. (Dallas). ISBN 0-919123-25-2. 176 pp. $20

27. Phallos: Sacred Image of the Masculine
Eugene Monick (Scranton, PA). ISBN 0-919123-26-0. 144 pp. $18

28. The Christian Archetype: A Jungian Commentary on the Life of Christ
Edward F. Edinger (Los Angeles). ISBN 0-919123-27-9. 144 pp. $18

30. Touching: Body Therapy and Depth Psychology
Deldon Anne McNeely (Lynchburg, VA). ISBN 0-919123-29-5. 128 pp. $18

31. Personality Types: Jung's Model of Typology
Daryl Sharp (Toronto). ISBN 0-919123-30-9. 128 pp. $18

32. The Sacred Prostitute: Eternal Aspect of the Feminine
Nancy Qualls-Corbett (Birmingham). ISBN 0-919123-31-7. 176 pp. $20

33. When the Spirits Come Back
Janet O. Dallett (Seal Harbor, WA). ISBN 0-919123-32-5. 160 pp. $18

34. The Mother: Archetypal Image in Fairy Tales
Sibylle Birkhäuser-Oeri (Zürich). ISBN 0-919123-33-3. 176 pp. $20

35. The Survival Papers: Anatomy of a Midlife Crisis
Daryl Sharp (Toronto). ISBN 0-919123-34-1. 160 pp. $18

37. Dear Gladys: The Survival Papers, Book 2
Daryl Sharp (Toronto). ISBN 0-919123-36-8. 144 pp. $18

39. Acrobats of the Gods: Dance and Transformation
Joan Dexter Blackmer (Wilmot Flat, NH). ISBN 0-919123-38-4. 128 pp. $18

40. Eros and Pathos: Shades of Love and Suffering
Aldo Carotenuto (Rome). ISBN 0-919123-39-2. 160 pp. $18

41. The Ravaged Bridegroom: Masculinity in Women
Marion Woodman (Toronto). ISBN 0-919123-42-2. 224 pp. $22

43. Goethe's *Faust:* Notes for a Jungian Commentary
Edward F. Edinger (Los Angeles). ISBN 0-919123-44-9. 112 pp. $18

44. The Dream Story: Everything You Wanted To Know
Donald Broadribb (Baker's Hill, Australia). ISBN 0-919123-45-7. 256 pp. $24

45. The Rainbow Serpent: Bridge to Consciousness
Robert L. Gardner (Toronto). ISBN 0-919123-46-5. 128 pp. $18

46. Circle of Care: Clinical Issues in Jungian Therapy
Warren Steinberg (New York). ISBN 0-919123-47-3. 160 pp. $18

47. Jung Lexicon: A Primer of Terms & Concepts
Daryl Sharp (Toronto). ISBN 0-919123-48-1. 160 pp. $18

48. Body and Soul: The Other Side of Illness
Albert Kreinheder (Los Angeles). ISBN 0-919123-49-X. 112 pp. $18

49. Animus Aeternus: Exploring the Inner Masculine
Deldon Anne McNeely (Lynchburg, VA). ISBN 0-919123-50-3. 192 pp. $20

50. Castration and Male Rage: The Phallic Wound
Eugene Monick (Scranton, PA). ISBN 0-919123-51-1. 144 pp. $18

51. Saturday's Child: Encounters with the Dark Gods
Janet O. Dallett (Seal Harbor, WA). ISBN 0-919123-52-X. 128 pp. $18

52. The Secret Lore of Gardening: Patterns of Male Intimacy
Graham Jackson (Toronto). ISBN 0-919123-53-8. 160 pp. $18

53. The Refiner's Fire: Memoirs of a German Girlhood
Sigrid R. McPherson (Los Angeles). ISBN 0-919123-54-6. 208 pp. $20

54. Transformation of the God-Image: Jung's *Answer to Job*
Edward F. Edinger (Los Angeles). ISBN 0-919123-55-4. 144 pp. $18

55. Getting to Know You: The Inside Out of Relationship
Daryl Sharp (Toronto). ISBN 0-919123-56-2. 128 pp. $18

56. A Strategy for a Loss of Faith: Jung's Proposal
John P. Dourley (Ottawa). ISBN 0-919123-57-0. 144 pp. $18

58. Conscious Femininity: Interviews with Marion Woodman
Introduction by Marion Woodman (Toronto). ISBN 0-919123-59-7. 160 pp. $18

59. The Middle Passage: From Misery to Meaning in Midlife
James Hollis (Houston). ISBN 0-919123-60-0. 128 pp. $18

61. Chicken Little: The Inside Story *(A Jungian Romance)*
Daryl Sharp (Toronto). ISBN 0-919123-62-7. 128 pp. $18

62. Coming To Age: The Croning Years and Late-Life Transformation
Jane R. Prétat (Providence, RI). ISBN 0-919123-63-5. 144 pp. $18

63. Under Saturn's Shadow: The Wounding and Healing of Men
James Hollis (Houston). ISBN 0-919123-64-3. 144 pp. $18

65. The Mystery of the Coniunctio: Alchemical Image of Transformation
Edward F. Edinger (Los Angeles). ISBN 0-919123-67-8. 112 pp. $18

**66. The Mysterium Lectures: A Journey through C.G. Jung's
*Mysterium Coniunctionis***
Edward F. Edinger (Los Angeles). ISBN 0-919123-66-X. 352 pp. $30

67. Who Am I, Really? Personality, Soul and Individuation
Daryl Sharp (Toronto). ISBN 0-919123-68-6. 144 pp. $18

68. Tracking the Gods: The Place of Myth in Modern Life
James Hollis (Houston). ISBN 0-919123-69-4. 160 pp. $18

69. Melville's *Moby-Dick:* An American Nekyia
Edward F. Edinger (Los Angeles). ISBN 0-919123-70-8. 160 pp. $18

70. Psyche in Scripture: The Idea of the Chosen One and Other Essays
Rivkah Schärf Kluger (Israel). ISBN 0-919123-71-6. 128 pp. $18

71. The Aion Lectures: Exploring the Self in C.G. Jung's *Aion*
Edward F. Edinger (Los Angeles). ISBN 0-919123-72-4. 208 pp. $20

72. Living Jung: The Good and the Better
Daryl Sharp (Toronto). ISBN 0-919123-73-2. 128 pp. $18

73. Swamplands of the Soul: New Life in Dismal Places
James Hollis (Houston). ISBN 0-919123-74-0. 160 pp. $18

74. Food and Transformation: Imagery and Symbolism of Eating
Eve Jackson (London). ISBN 0-919123-75-9. 128 pp. $18

75. Archetypes & Strange Attractors: The Chaotic World of Symbols
John R. Van Eenwyk (Olympia, WA). ISBN 0-919123-76-7. 192 pp. $20

76. Archetypal Patterns in Fairy Tales
Marie-Louise von Franz (Zurich). ISBN 0-919123-77-5. 192 pp. $20

77. C.G. Jung: His Myth in Our Time
Marie-Louise von Franz (Zurich). ISBN 0-919123-78-3. 368 pp. $30

78. Divine Tempest: The Hurricane As a Psychic Phenomenon
David E. Schoen (New Orleans). ISBN 0-919123-79-1. 128 pp. $18

79. The Eden Project: In Search of the Magical Other
James Hollis (Houston). ISBN 0-919123-80-5. 160 pp. $18

80. Jungian Psychology Unplugged: My Life As an Elephant
Daryl Sharp (Toronto). ISBN 0-919123-81-3. 160 pp. $18

82. Now or Neverland: Peter Pan and the Myth of Eternal Youth
Ann Yeoman (Toronto). ISBN 0-919123-83-X. 192 pp. $20

83. The Cat: A Tale of Feminine Redemption
Marie-Louise von Franz (Zurich). ISBN 0-919123-84-8. 160 pp. $18

84. Celebrating Soul: Preparing for the New Religion
Lawrence W. Jaffe (Berkeley, CA). ISBN 0-919123-85-6. 128 pp. $18

85. The Psyche in Antiquity, Book 1: Early Greek Philosophy
Edward F. Edinger (Los Angeles). ISBN 0-919123-86-4. 128 pp. $18

86. The Psyche in Antiquity, Book 2: Gnosticism and Early Christianity
Edward F. Edinger (Los Angeles). ISBN 0-919123-87-2. 160 pp. $18

87. The Problem of the Puer Aeternus
Marie-Louise von Franz (Zurich). ISBN 0-919123-88-0. 288 pp. $25

88. The Inner Journey: Lectures and Essays on Jungian Psychology
Barbara Hannah (Zurich). ISBN 0-919123-89-9. 160 pp. $18

89. Aurora Consurgens: A Document Attributed to Thomas Aquinas
Commentary by Marie-Louise von Franz (Zurich). ISBN 0-919123-90-2. 576 pp. $45

90. Ego and Self: The Old Testament Prophets
Edward F. Edinger (Los Angeles). ISBN 0-919123-91-0. 160 pp. $18

92. Creating a Life: Finding Your Individual Path
James Hollis (Houston). ISBN 0-919123-93-7. 160 pp. $18

94. Jung and Yoga: The Psyche-Body Connection
Judith Harris (London, Ontario) ISBN 0-919123-95-3. 160 pp. $18

95. Digesting Jung: Food for the Journey
Daryl Sharp (Toronto). ISBN 0-919123-96-1. 128 pp. $18

97. Animal Guides in Life, Myth and Dreams
Neil Russack (San Francisco). ISBN 0-919123-98-8. 224 pp. $22

99. The Secret World of Drawings
Gregg M. Furth (New York). ISBN 1-894574-00-1. 176 pp. $25

111. The Secret Garden: Temenos for Individuation
Margaret Eileen Meredith (Toronto) ISBN 1-894574-12-5. 160 pp. $18

112. Not the Big Sleep: On having fun, seriously *(A Jungian Romance)*
Daryl Sharp (Toronto) ISBN 1-894574-13-3. 128 pp. $18

113. The Use of Dreams in Couple Counseling
Renée Nell (Litchfield, CT). ISBN 1-894574-14-1. 160 pp. $18

Discounts: any 3-5 books, 10%; 6-9 books, 20%; 10 or more, 25%

Add Postage/Handling: 1-2 books, $6; 3-4 books, $8; 5-9 books, $15; 10 or more, $10

Credit cards: Contact BookWorld toll-free: 1-800-444-2524, or Fax 1-800-777-2525

Free **Catalogue** describing over **100** titles, and **Jung at Heart** newsletter

INNER CITY BOOKS, Box 1271, Station Q, Toronto, ON M4T 2P4, Canada
Tel. 416-927-0355 / Fax: 416-924-1814 / E-mail: sales@innercitybooks.net